Folksongs *for* Accordion

Arranged by Gary Meisner

ISBN 978-1-4768-0600-6

HAL•LEONARD®
CORPORATION
7777 W. BLUEMOUND RD. P.O. BOX 13819 MILWAUKEE, WI 53213

In Australia Contact:
Hal Leonard Australia Pty. Ltd.
4 Lentara Court
Cheltenham, Victoria, 3192 Australia
Email: ausadmin@halleonard.com.au

Visit Hal Leonard Online at
www.halleonard.com

CONTENTS

THE CAMPBELLS ARE COMING

Scottish Folksong

*Both bass notes

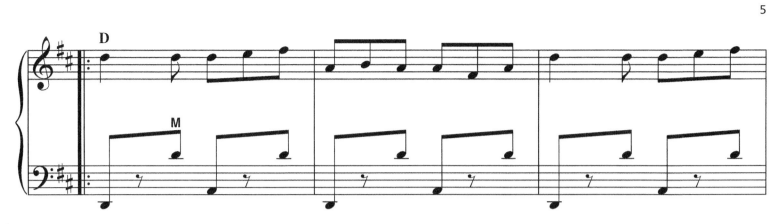

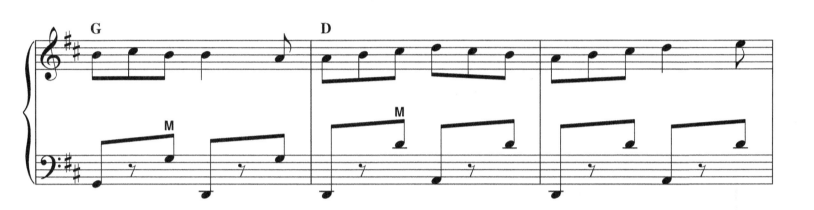

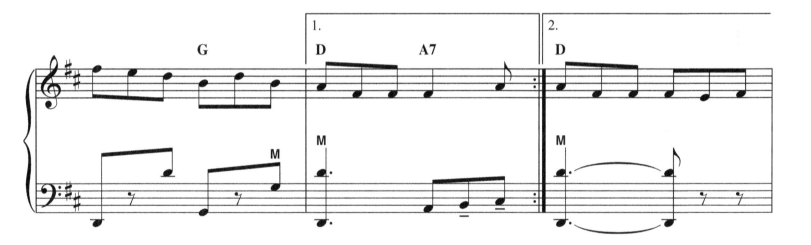

CIELITO LINDO
(My Pretty Darling)

By C. FERNANDEZ

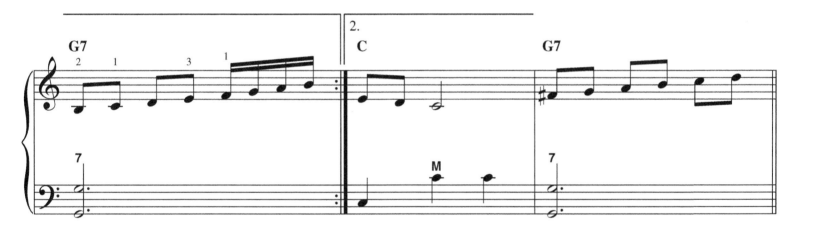

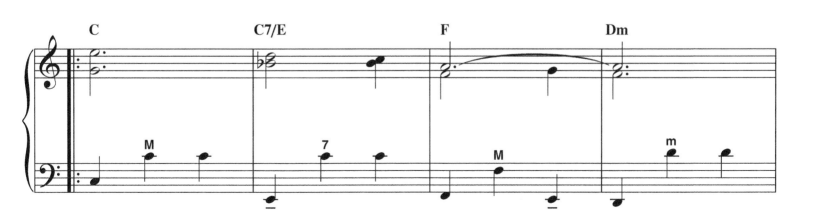

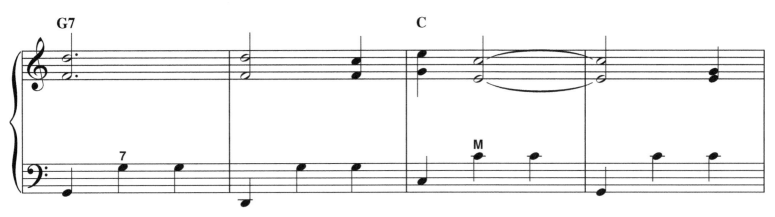

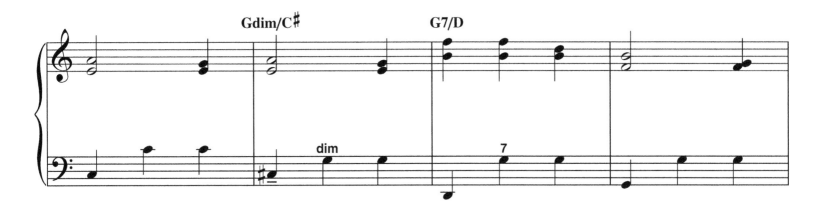

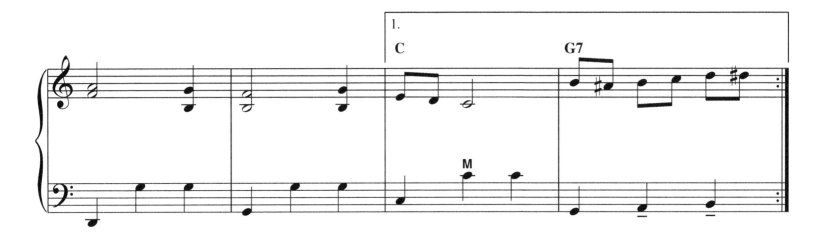

THE CRAWDAD SONG

Traditional

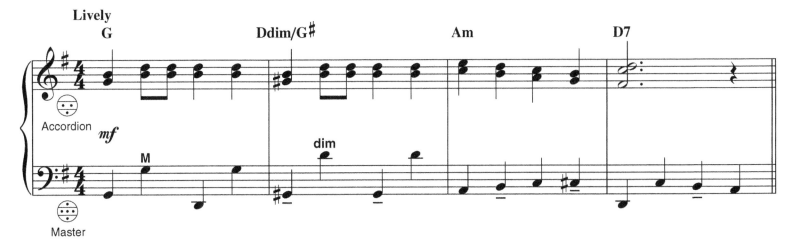

You get a line and I'll get a pole, ___ hon-ey.
Get up, old man, you slept too ___ late, ___ hon-ey.

You get a line and I'll get a pole, ___
Get up, old man, you slept too ___ late, ___

babe. ___
babe. ___

You get a line and
Get up, old man, you

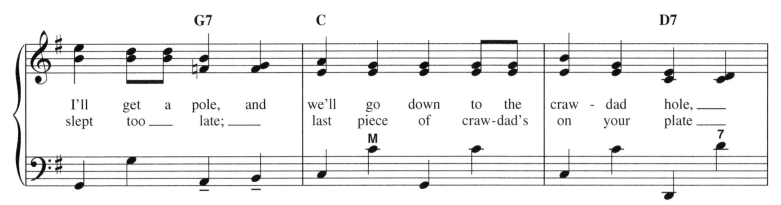

I'll get a pole, and we'll go down to the craw-dad hole, ____
slept too ____ late; ____ last piece of craw-dad's on your plate ____

1.

hon - ey, sug-ar ba - by, mine.
hon - ey, sug-ar ba - by

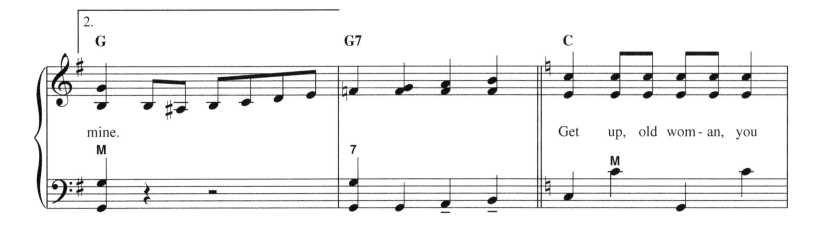

2.

mine. Get up, old wom-an, you

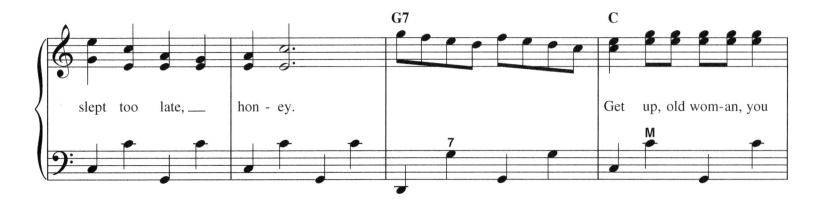

slept too late, ___ hon - ey. Get up, old wom-an, you

11

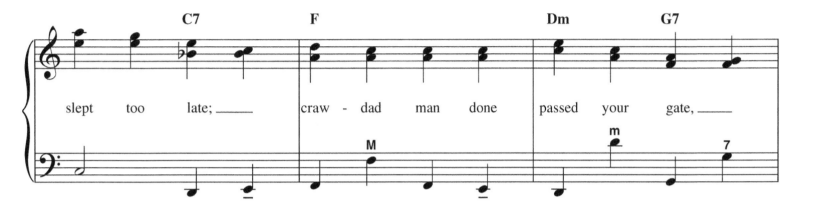

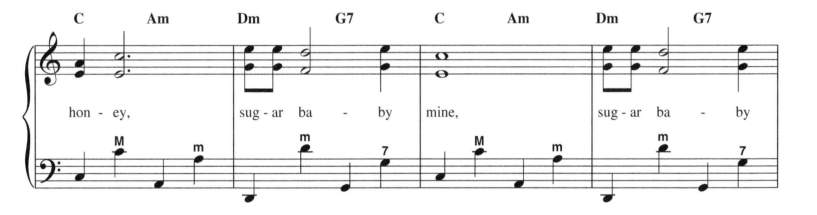

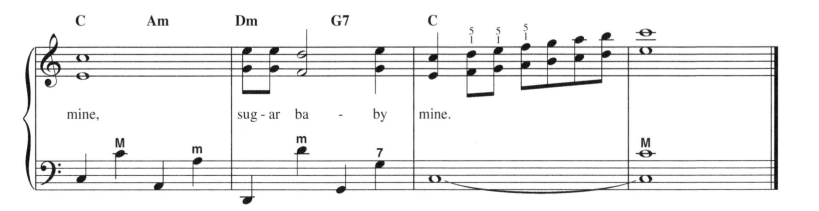

DANNY BOY
featured in the Television Series THE DANNY THOMAS SHOW

Words by FREDERICK EDWARD WEATHERLY
Traditional Irish Folk Melody

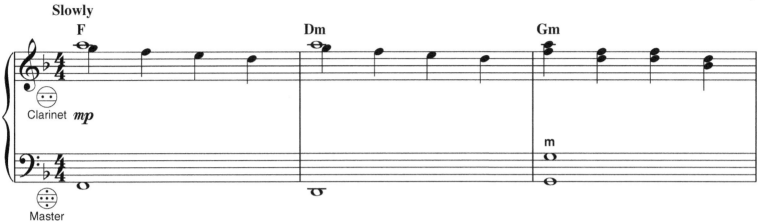

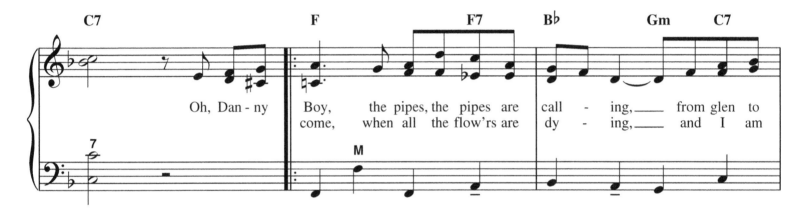

Oh, Dan - ny Boy, the pipes, the pipes are call - ing,____ from glen to
come, when all the flow'rs are dy - ing,____ and I am

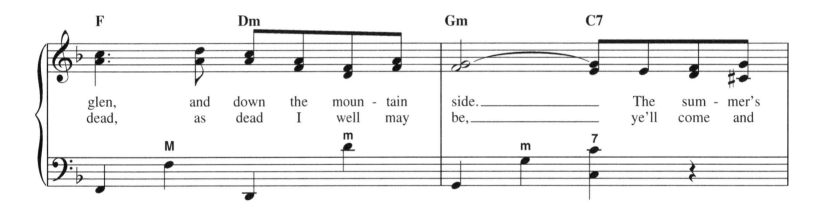

glen, and down the moun - tain side.____ The sum - mer's
dead, as dead I well may be,____ ye'll come and

gone, and all the ros - es fall - ing,____ It's you, it's you must go and I must
find the place where I am ly - ing,____ and kneel and say an *A - ve* there for

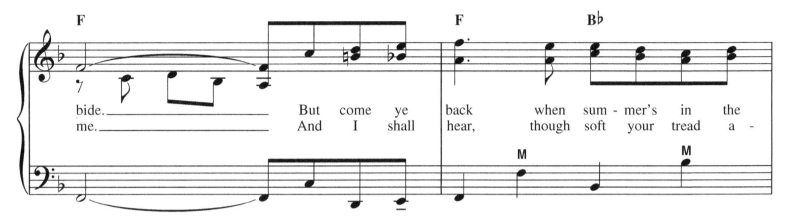

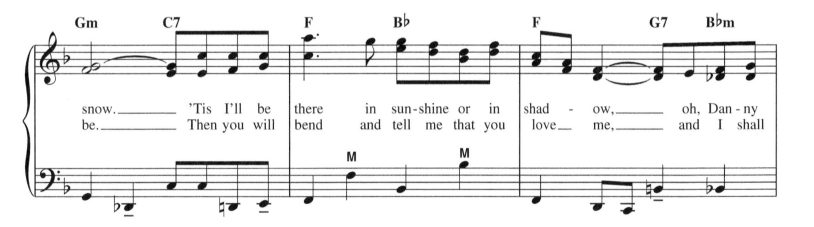

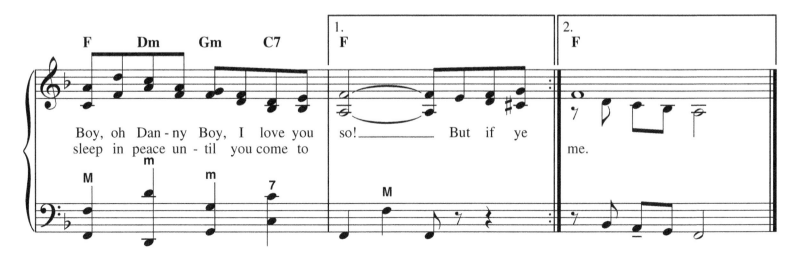

DU, DU LIEGST MIR IM HERZEN

(You, You Weigh on My Heart)

German Folksong

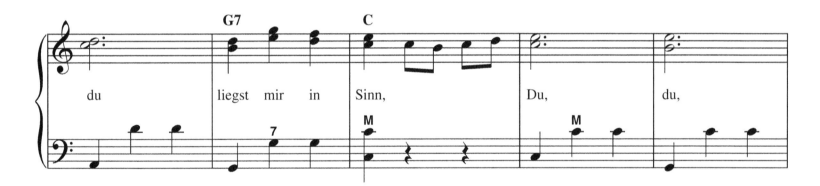

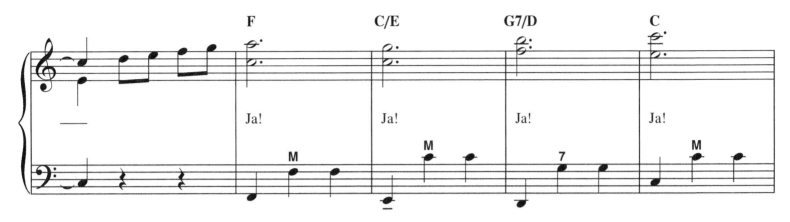

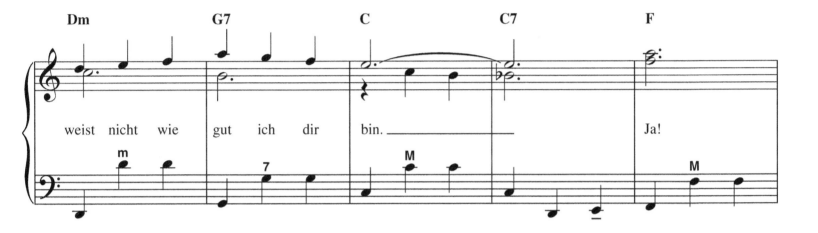

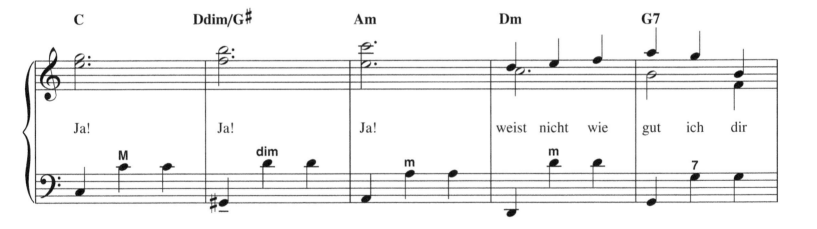

FLOW GENTLY, SWEET AFTON

Lyrics by ROBERT BURNS
Music by ALEXANDER HUME

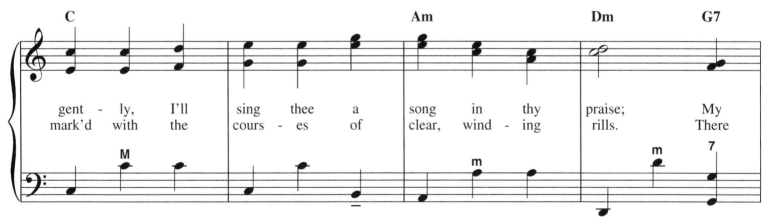

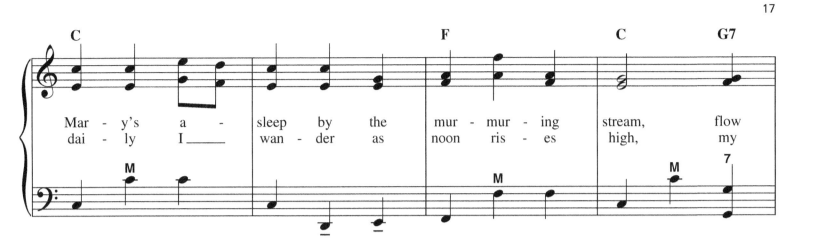

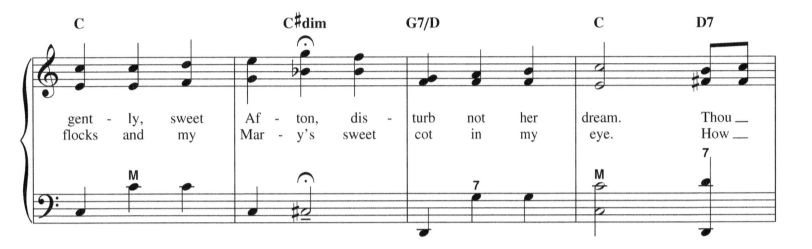

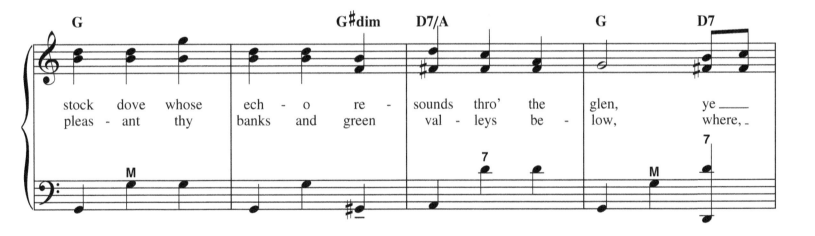

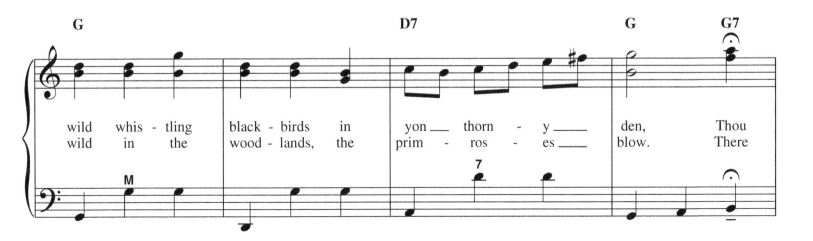

Additional lyrics

3. Thy crystal stream, Afton, how lovely it glides,
   And winds by the cot where my Mary resides.
   How wanton thy waters her snowy feet lave,
   As, gath'ring sweet flow'rets, she stems thy clear wave.
   Flow gently, sweet Afton, among thy green braes,
   Flow gently, sweet river, the theme of my lays.
   My Mary's asleep by thy murmuring stream.
   Flow gently, sweet Afton, disturb not her dreams.

GUANTANAMERA

Cuban Folksong

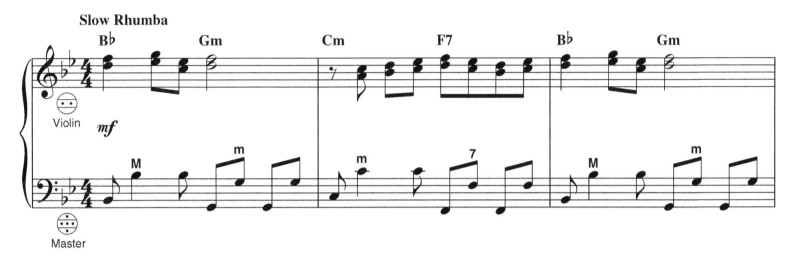

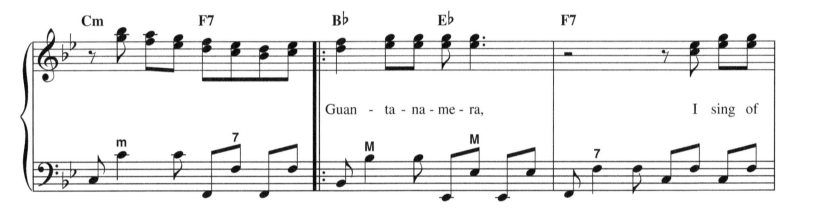

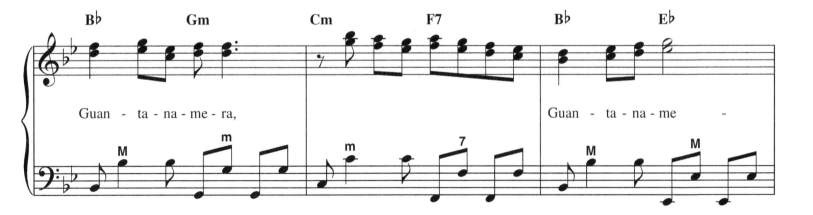

ra, I sing of Guan - ta - na - me - ra, { I come from
{ With all the

where palm trees flour - ish, to speak the
poor and the hum - ble I cast my

truth's my de - si - re. I come from
fate and de - vo - tion. With all the

where palm trees flour - ish, to speak the
poor and the hum - ble I cast my

truth's _____ my de - si - re. And I must sing or I per -
fate _____ and de - vo - tion. The moun-tain streams as they tum -

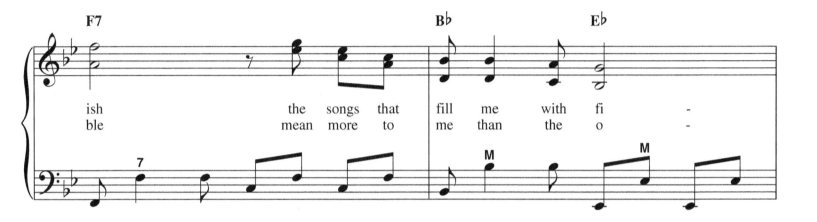

ish the songs that fill me with fi -
ble mean more to me than with the o -

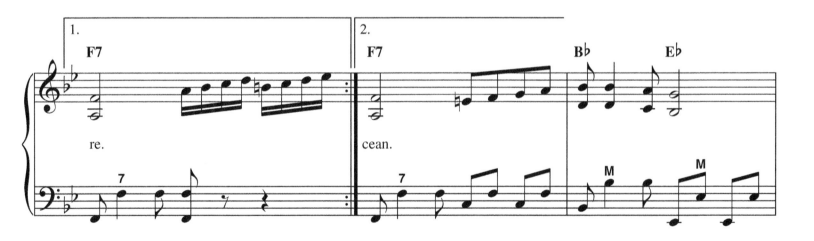

1.
re.

2.
cean.

GREENSLEEVES

Sixteenth Century Traditional English

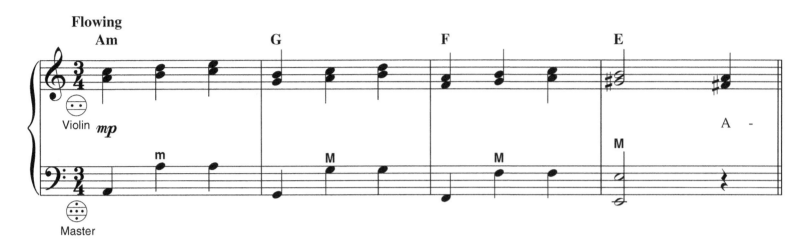

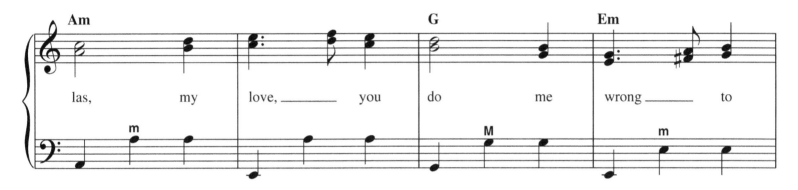

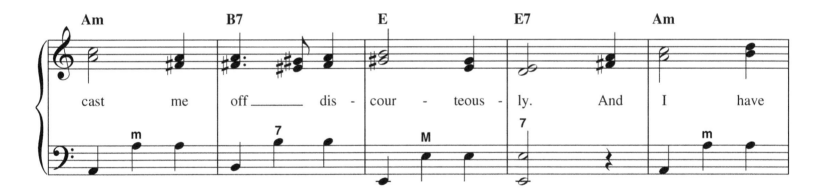

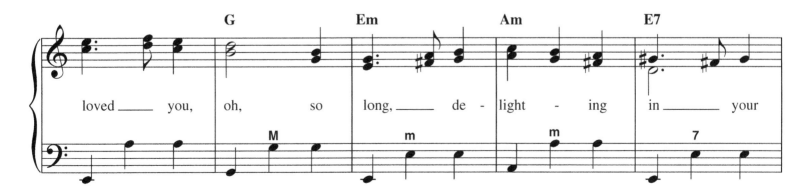

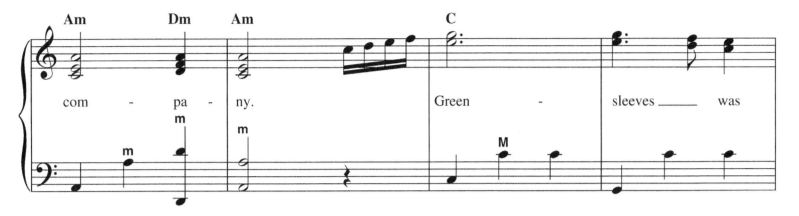

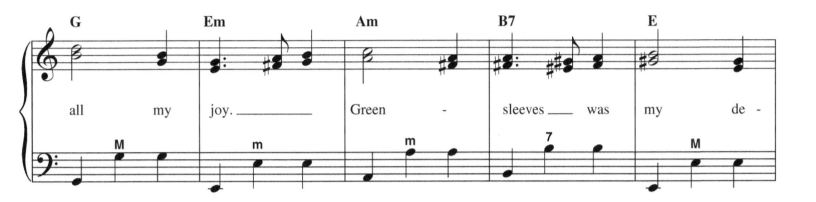

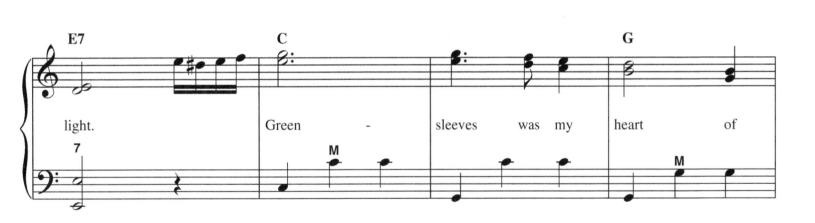

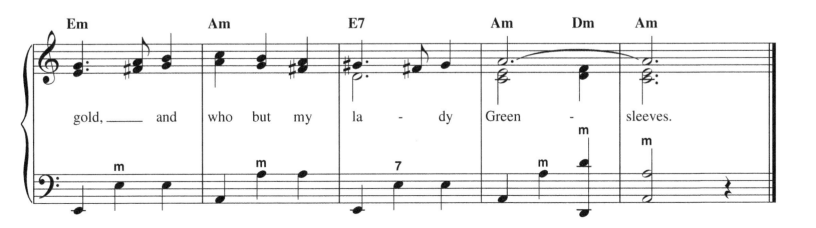

HE'S GOT THE WHOLE WORLD IN HIS HANDS

Traditional Spiritual

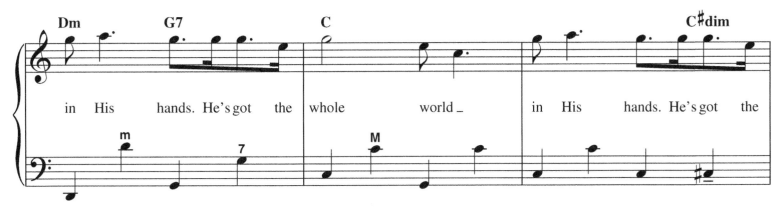

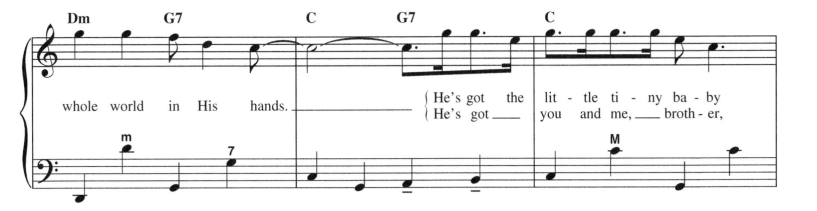

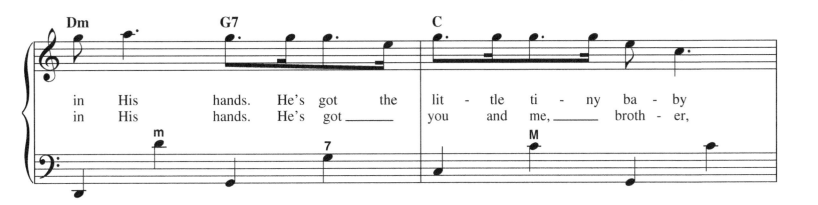

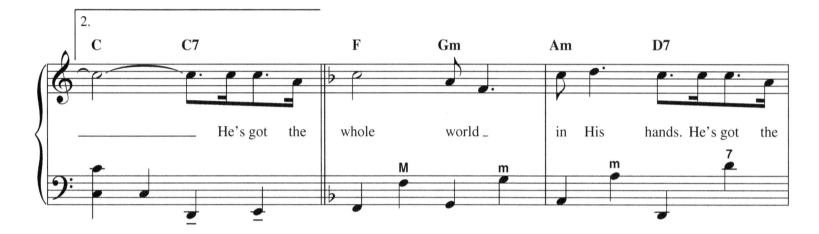

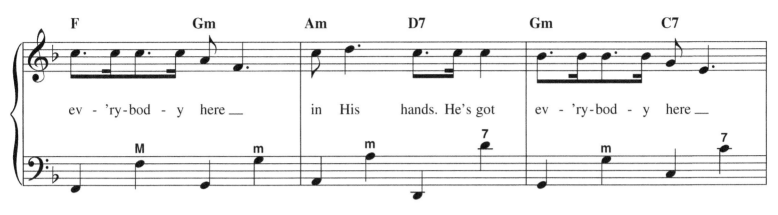

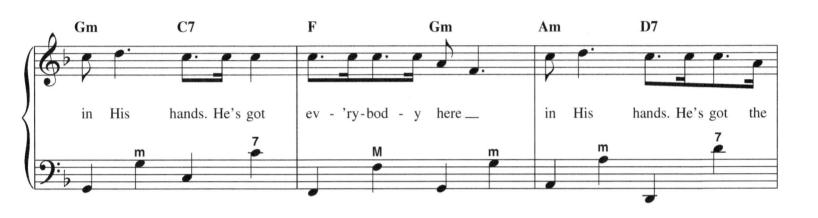

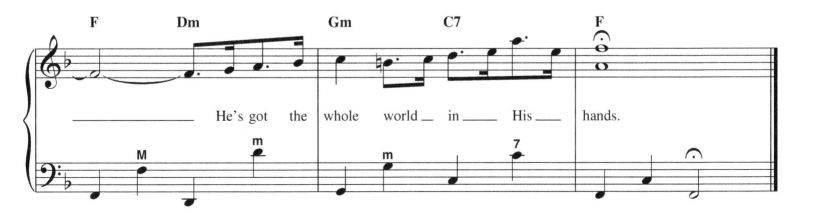

HOUSE OF THE RISING SUN

Southern American Folksong

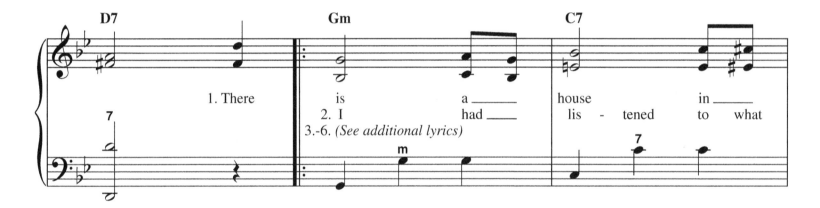

1. There is a _____ house in _____
2. I had _____ lis - tened to what
3.-6. *(See additional lyrics)*

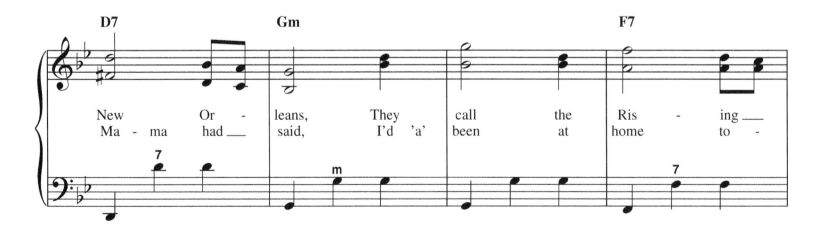

New Or - leans, They call the Ris - ing _____
Ma - ma had _____ said, I'd 'a' been at home to -

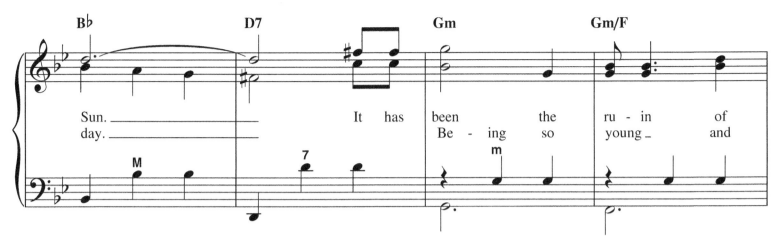

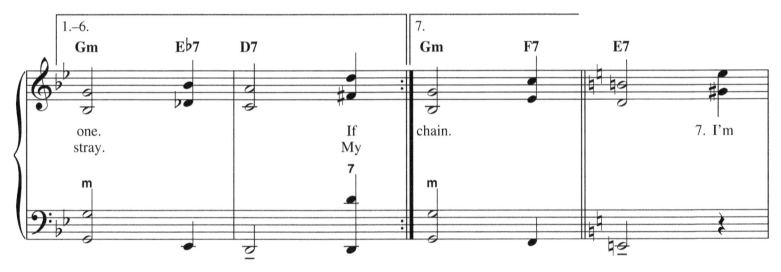

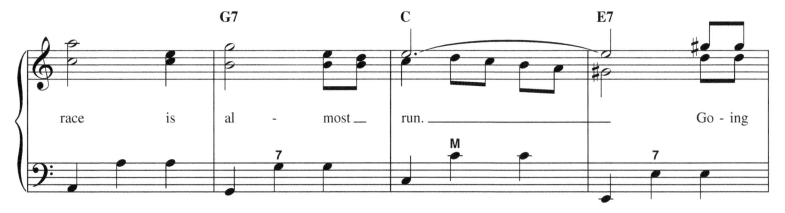

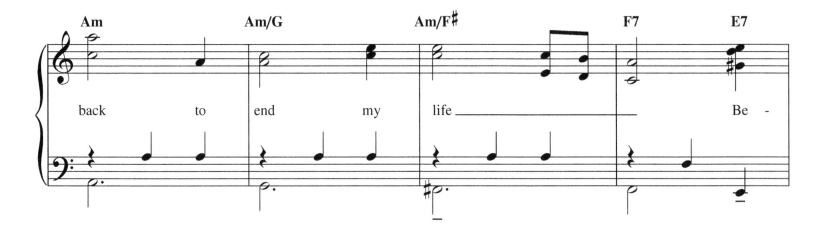

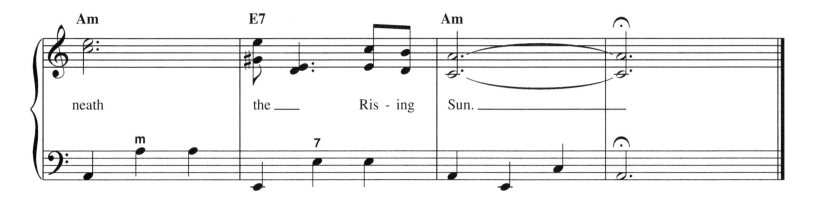

Additional Lyrics

3. My mother, she's a tailor, she sells those new blue jeans.
   My sweetheart, he's a drunkard, Lord, drink down in New Orleans.

4. The only thing a drunkard needs is a suitcase and a trunk.
   The only time he's satisfied is when he's on a drunk.

5. Go tell my baby, sister, never do like I have done.
   To shun that house in New Orleans, they call the Rising Sun.

6. One foot is on the platform, and the other is on the train.
   I'm going back to New Orleans to wear the ball and chain.

LA CUCARACHA

Mexican Revolutionary Folksong

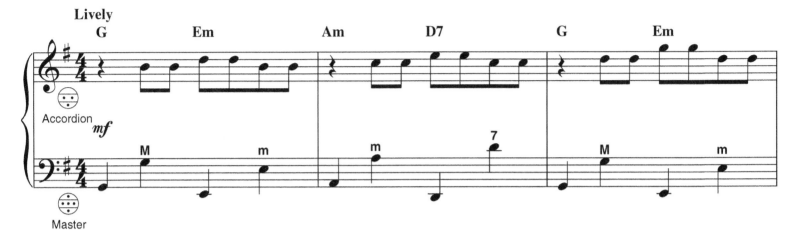

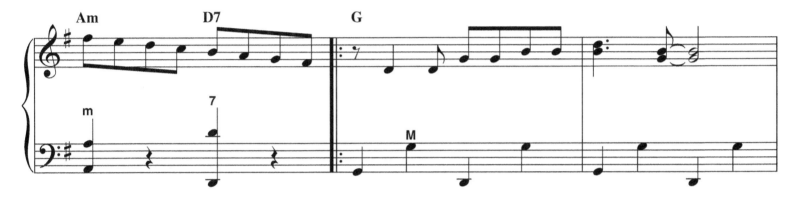

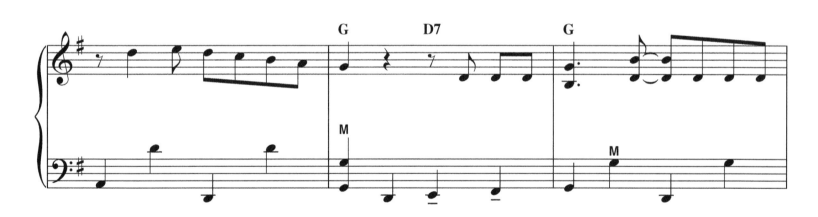

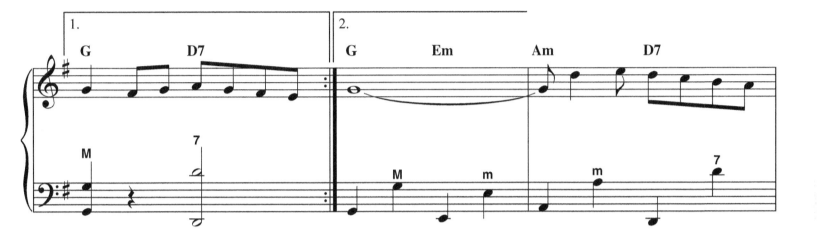

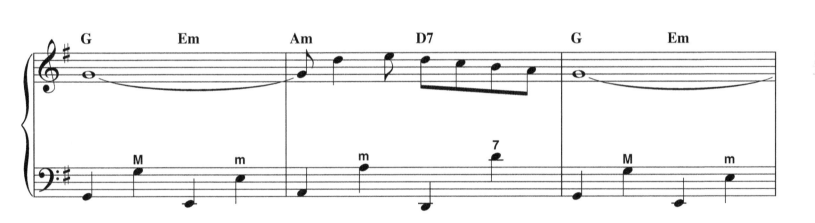

I GAVE MY LOVE A CHERRY
(The Riddle Song)

Traditional

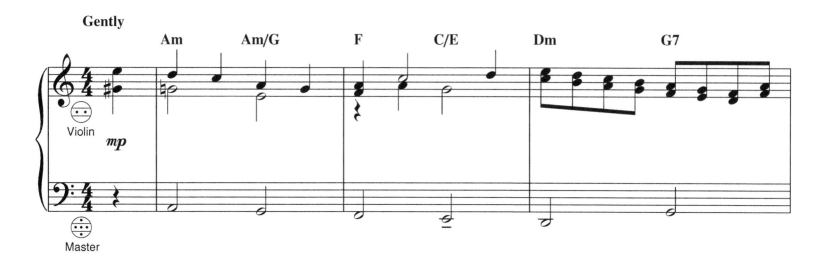

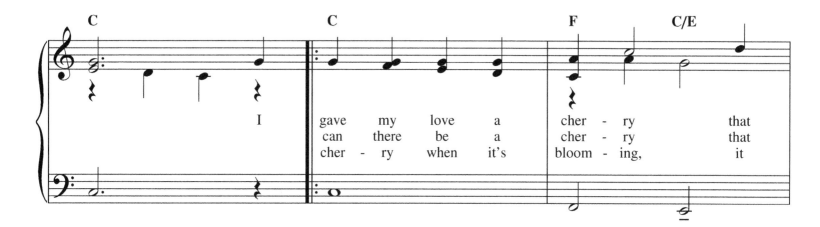

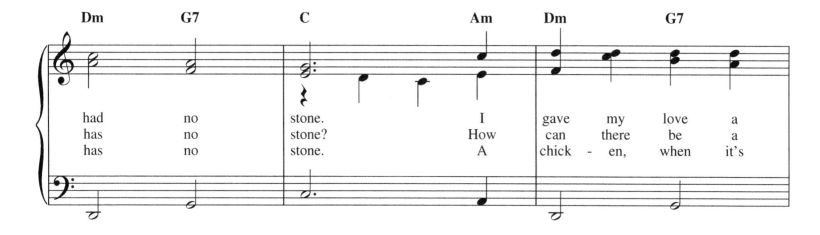

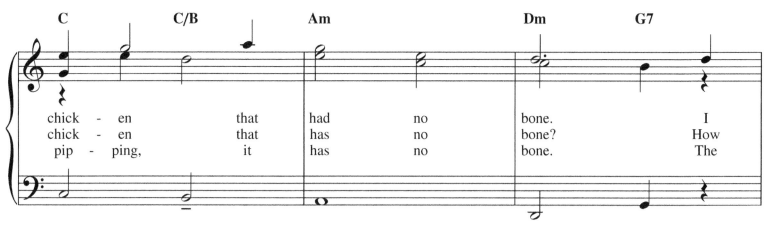

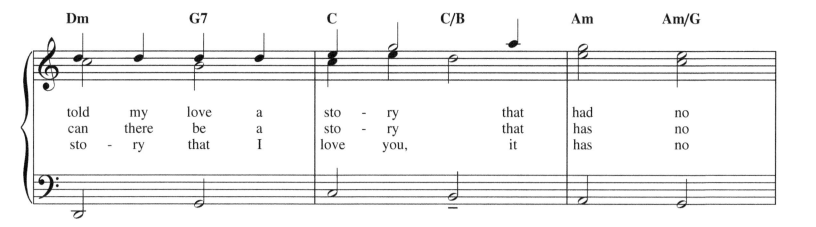

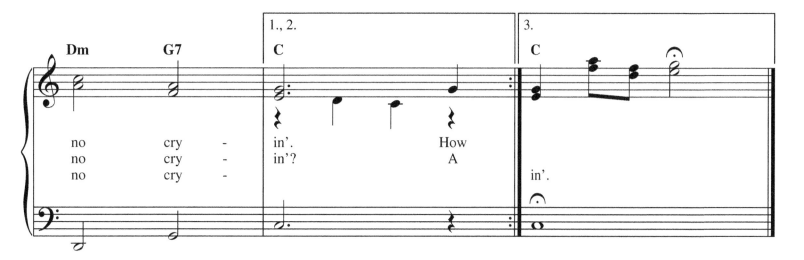

THE IRISH WASHERWOMAN

Irish Folksong

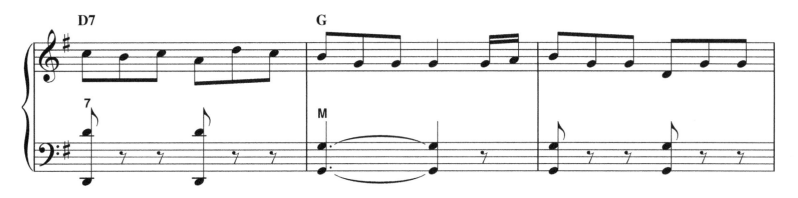

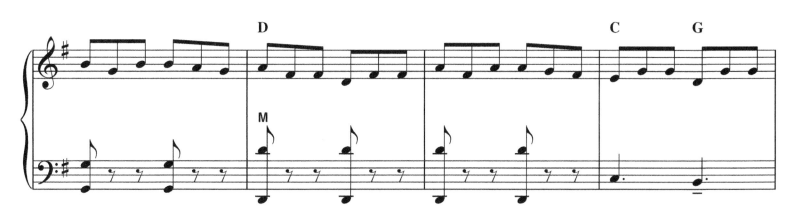

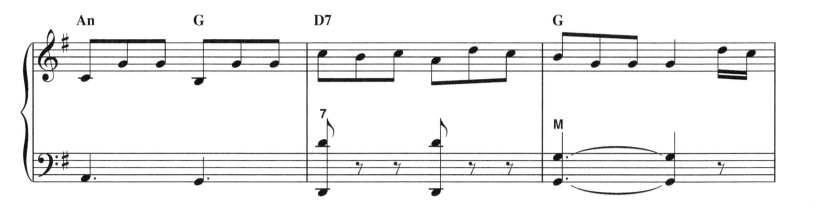

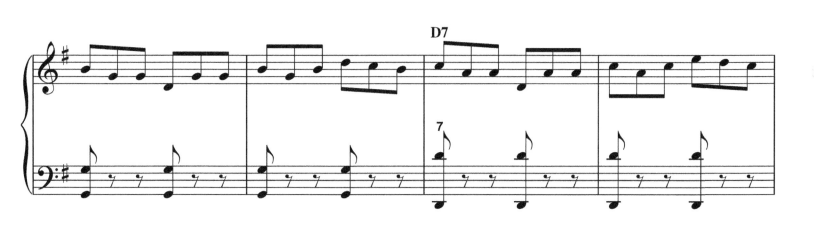

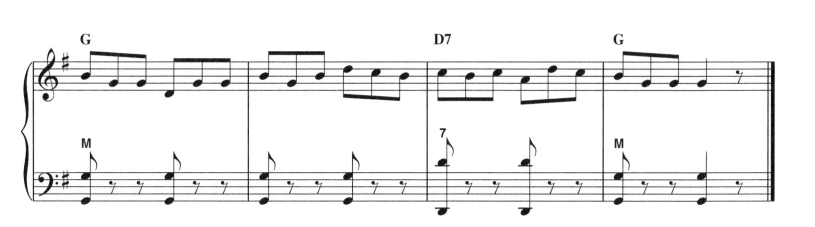

JOSHUA
(Fit the Battle of Jericho)

African-American Spiritual

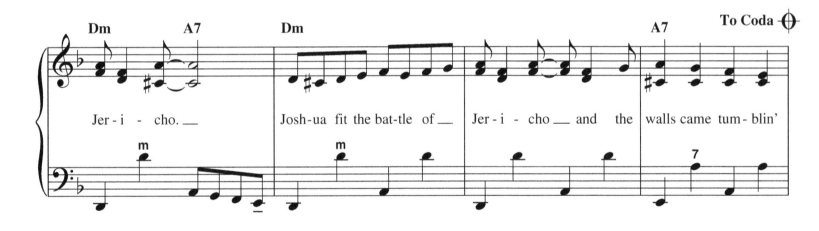

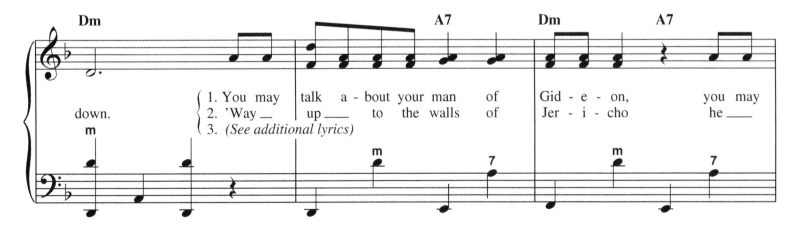

Additional Lyrics

3. Then the lamb, ram, sheep horns began to blow
   And the trumpets began to sound;
   And Joshua commanded the children to shout
   And the walls came tumblin' down.

JUST A CLOSER WALK WITH THEE

Traditional
Arranged by KENNETH MORRIS

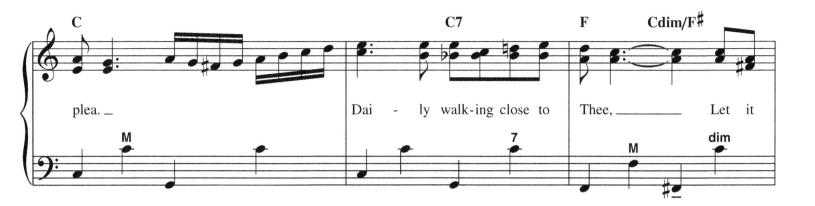

Additional Lyrics

3. When my feeble life is o'er,
   Time for me will be no more.
   Guide me gently, safely o'er
   To Thy kingdom shore, to Thy shore.
   Chorus

THE MAN ON THE FLYING TRAPEZE

Words by GEORGE LEYBOURNE
Music by ALFRED LEE

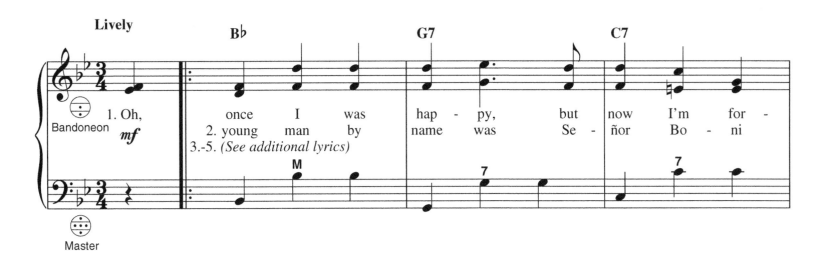

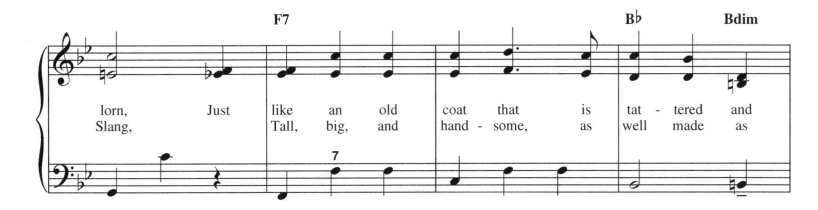

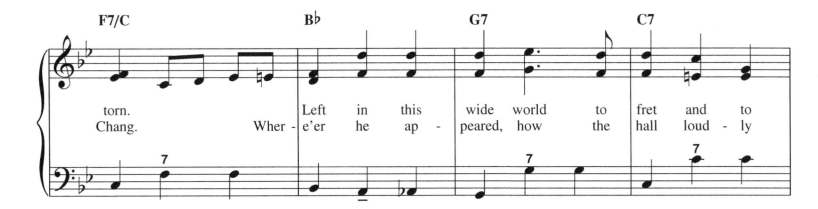

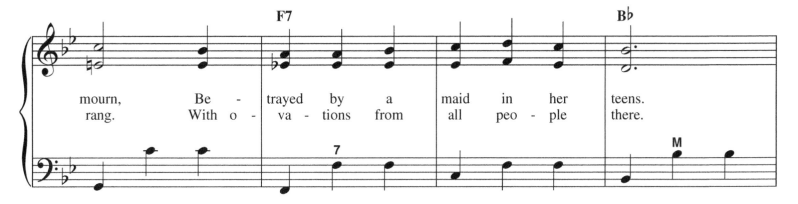

mourn, Be - trayed by a maid in her teens.
rang. With o - va - tions from all peo - ple there.

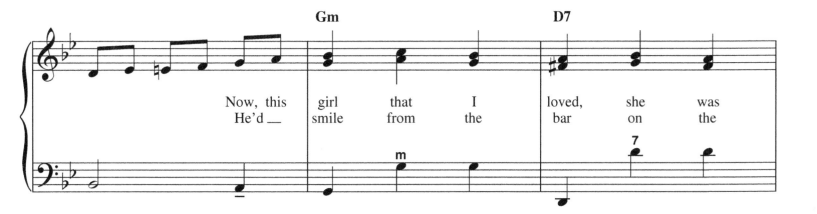

Now, this girl that I loved, she was
He'd — smile that from I the bar on was the

hand - some, And I tried all I knew her to
peo - ple be - low And — one night he smiled on my

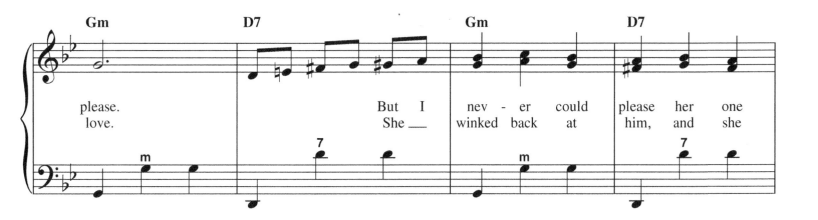

please. But I nev - er could please her one
love. She — winked back at him, and she

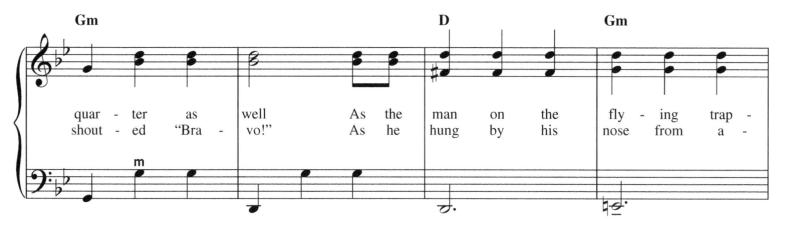

quar - ter as well As the man on the fly - ing trap -
shout - ed "Bra - vo!" As he hung by his nose from a -

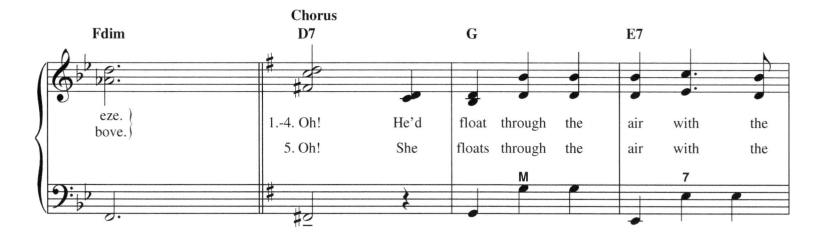

Chorus

eze.
bove.

1.-4. Oh! He'd float through the air with the
5. Oh! She floats through the air with the

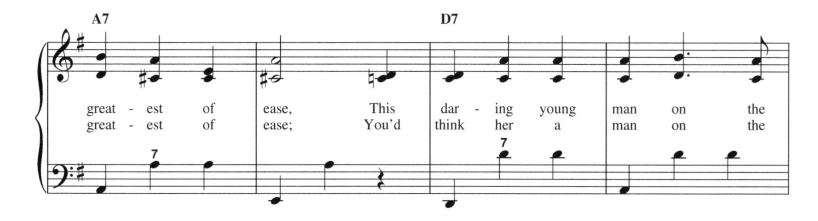

great - est of ease, This dar - ing young man on the
great - est of ease; You'd think her a man on the

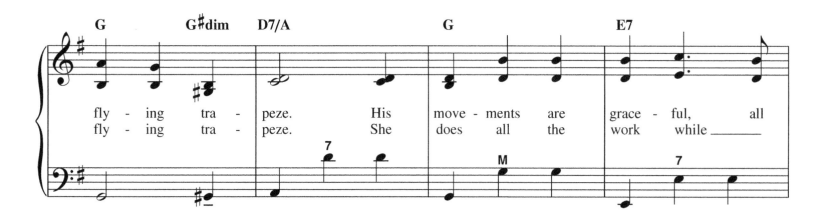

fly - ing tra - peze. His move - ments are grace - ful, all
fly - ing tra - peze. She does all the work while _____

girls he does please, And my love he has pur - loined a -
he takes his ease, And ___ that's what's be - come of my

way.

Now the

love.

Additional Lyrics

3. Her father and mother were both on my side,
   And tried very hard to make her my bride.
   Her father, he sighed, and her mother, she cried
   To see her throw herself away.
   'Twas all no avail, she went there ev'ry night
   And threw her bouquets on the stage,
   Which caused him to meet her; how he ran me down,
   To tell it would take a whole page.
   Chorus

4. One night I as usual went to her dear home,
   And found there her mother and father alone,
   I asked for my love, and soon 'twas made known,
   To my horror, that she'd run away.
   She packed up her boxes and eloped in the night
   With him, with the greatest of ease.
   From two stories high he had lowered her down
   To the ground on his flying trapeze.
   Chorus

5. Some months after that I went into a hall;
   To my surprise I found there on the wall
   A bill in red letters which did my heart gall,
   That she was appearing with him.
   He'd taught her gymnastics and dressed her in tights
   To help him live at ease.
   He'd made her assume a masculine name,
   And now she goes on the trapeze.
   Chorus

MOLLY MALONE
(Cockles & Mussels)

Irish Folksong

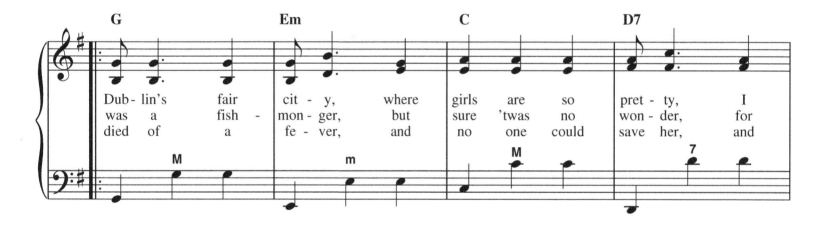

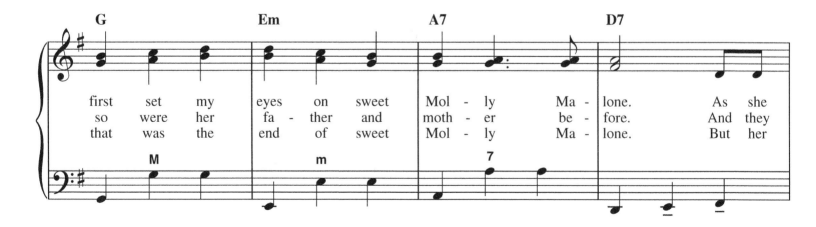

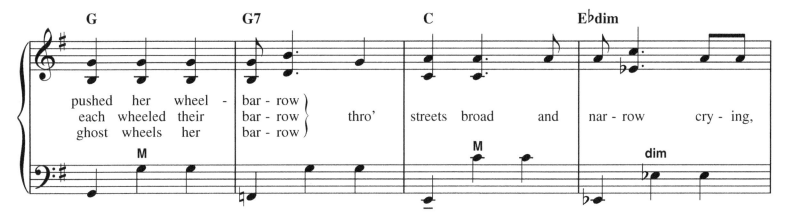

pushed her wheel - bar - row
each wheeled their bar - row } thro' streets broad and nar - row cry - ing,
ghost wheels her bar - row

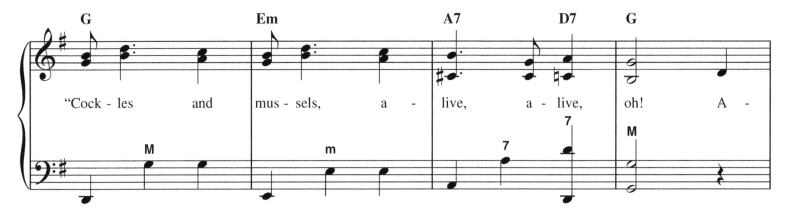

"Cock - les and mus - sels, a - live, a - live, oh! A -

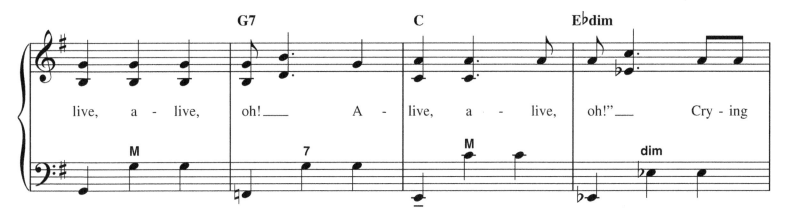

live, a - live, oh!___ A - live, a - live, oh!"___ Cry - ing

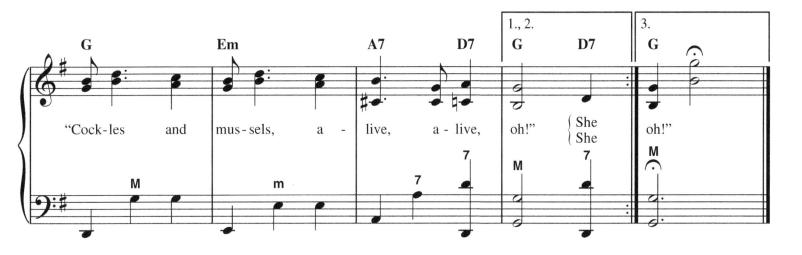

"Cock - les and mus - sels, a - live, a - live, oh!" { She / She } oh!"

MY BONNIE LIES OVER THE OCEAN

Traditional

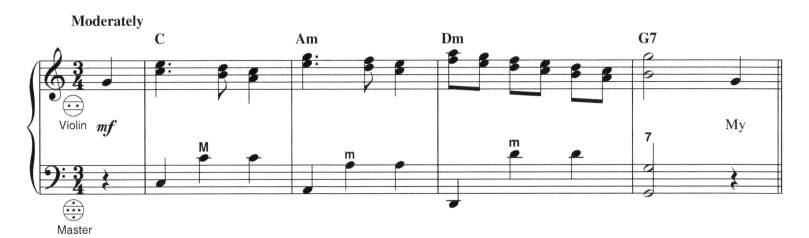

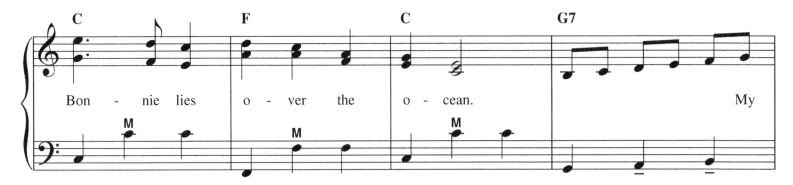

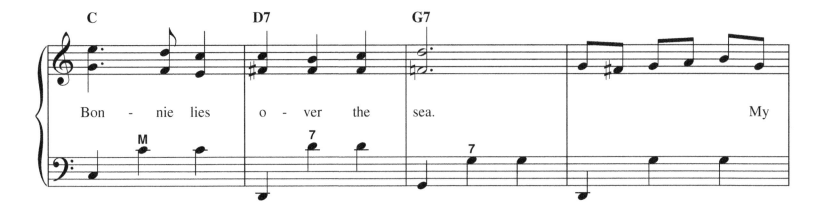

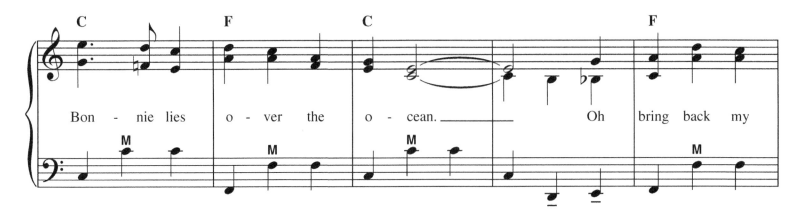

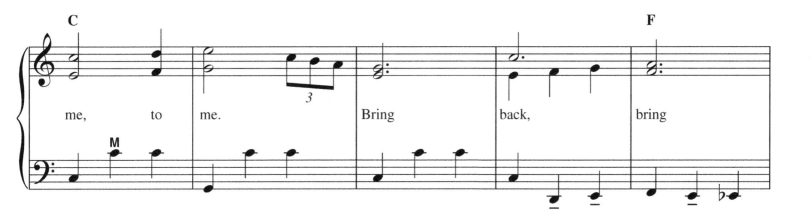

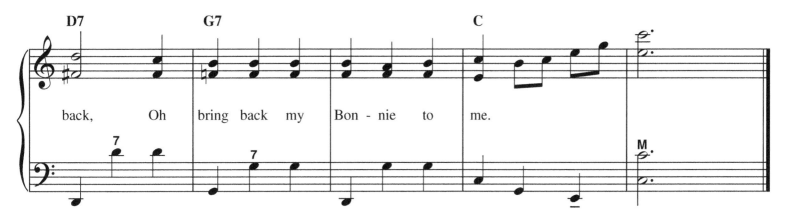

NOBODY KNOWS THE TROUBLE I'VE SEEN

African-American Spiritual

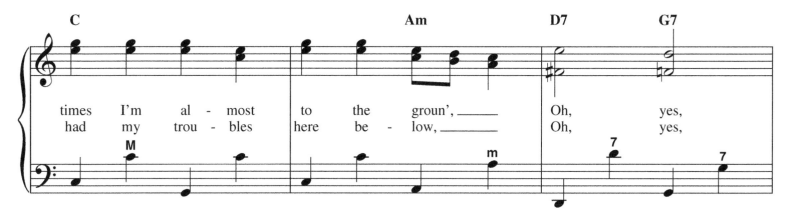

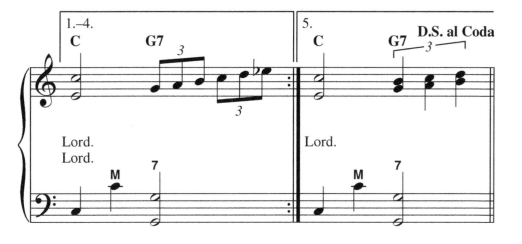

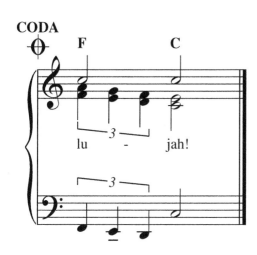

Additional Lyrics

3. One day when I was walkin' along,
   Oh, yes, Lord;
   The sky opened up and love come down,
   Oh, yes, Lord.

4. What made old satan hate me so?
   Oh, yes, Lord;
   He had me once and had to let me go,
   Oh, yes, Lord.

5. I never shall forget that day,
   Oh, yes, Lord;
   When Jesus washed my sins away,
   Oh, yes, Lord.

OH, THEM GOLDEN SLIPPERS

Words and Music by
JAMES A. BLAND

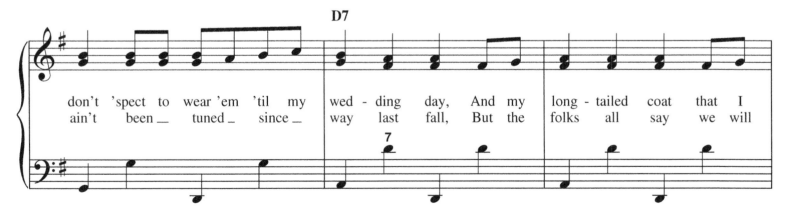

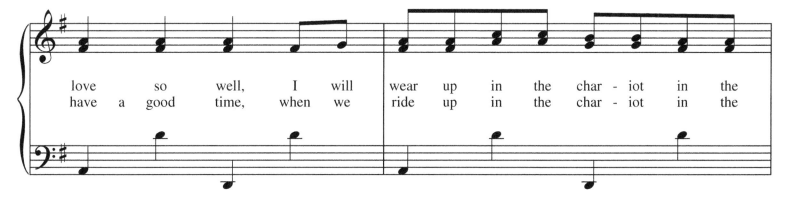

love   so   well,   I   will   wear   up   in   the   char - iot   in   the
have   a   good   time,   when   we   ride   up   in   the   char - iot   in   the

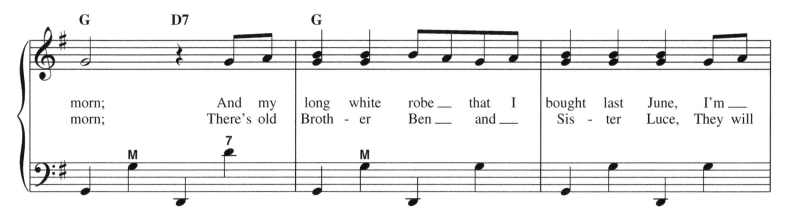

G　　　　**D7**　　　　**G**

morn;　　　And   my   long   white   robe ___   that   I   bought   last   June,   I'm ___
morn;　　　There's   old   Broth - er   Ben ___   and ___   Sis - ter   Luce,   They   will

　　　　　　　　　　　　　　　　　　　D7

goin'   to   get   changed   'case   it   fits   too   soon,   And   the
tel - e - graph   the   news   to   Un - cle   'Bac - co   Juice,   And   What   a

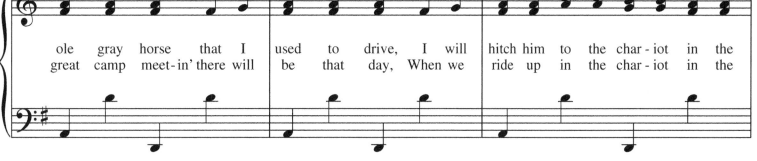

ole   gray   horse   that   I   used   to   drive,   I   will   hitch   him   to   the   char - iot   in   the
great   camp   meet-in'   there   will   be   that   day,   When   we   ride   up   in   the   char - iot   in   the

Chorus

morn.
morn.

Oh, them gold - en slip - pers!

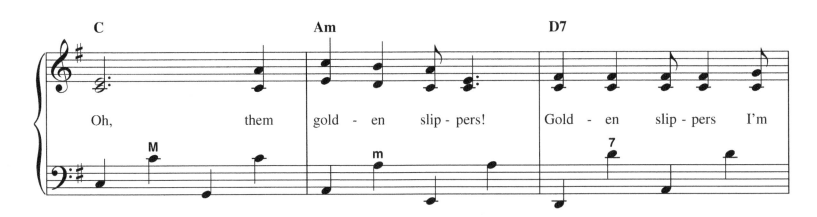

Oh, them gold - en slip - pers! Gold - en slip - pers I'm

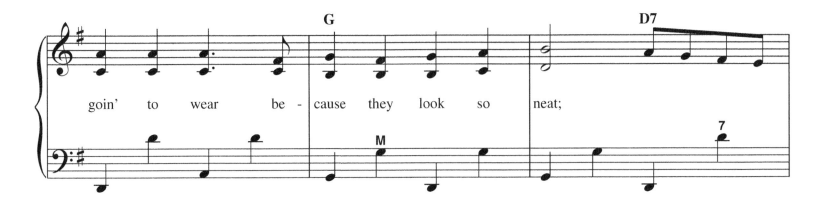

goin' to wear be - cause they look so neat;

Oh, them gold - en slip - pers! Oh, them

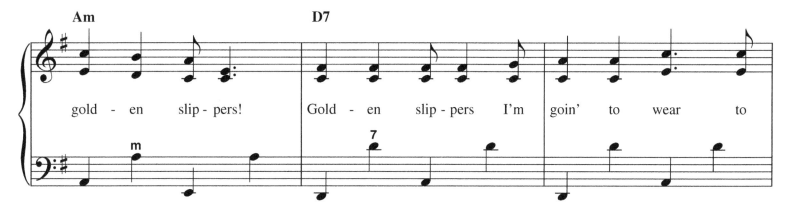

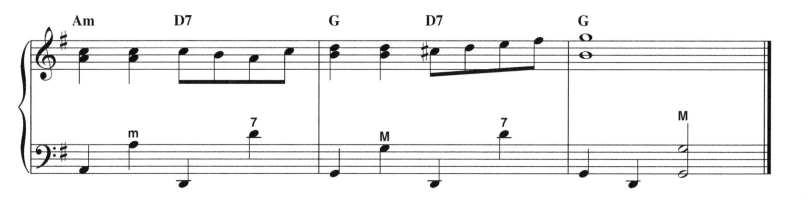

Additional Lyrics

3. So, it's goodbye children, I will have to go,
   Where the rain don't fall and the wind don't blow,
   And your ulster coats, why, you will not need,
   When you ride up in the chariot in the morn;
   But your golden slippers must be nice and clean,
   And our age must be just sweet sixteen,
   And your white kid gloves you will have to wear,
   When you ride up in the chariot in the morn.
   Chorus

SAILING, SAILING

Words and Music by
GODFREY MARKS

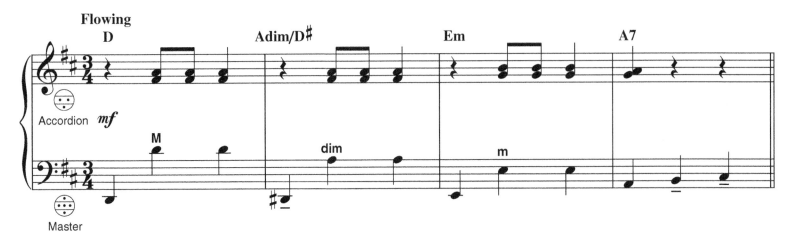

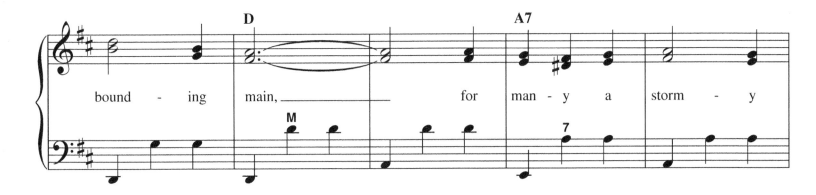

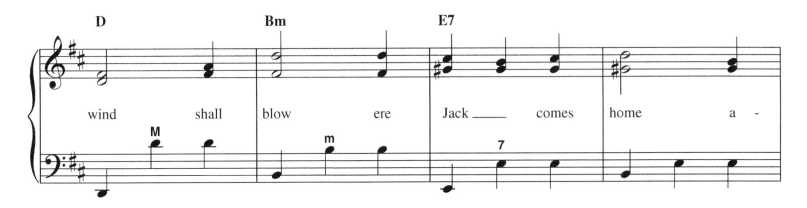

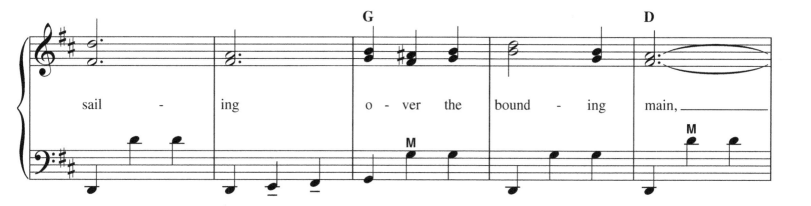

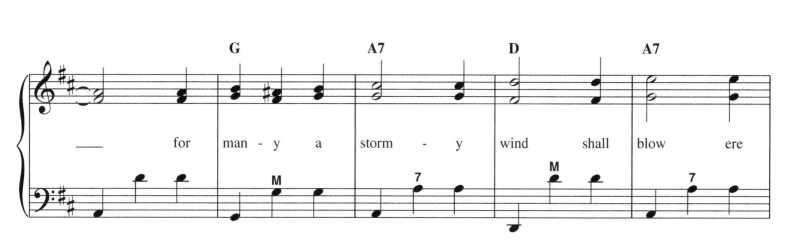

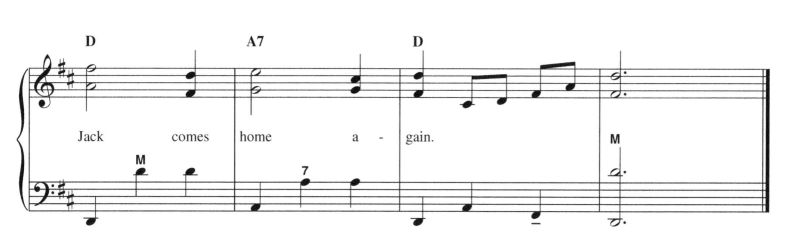

SANTA LUCIA

By TEODORO COTTRAU

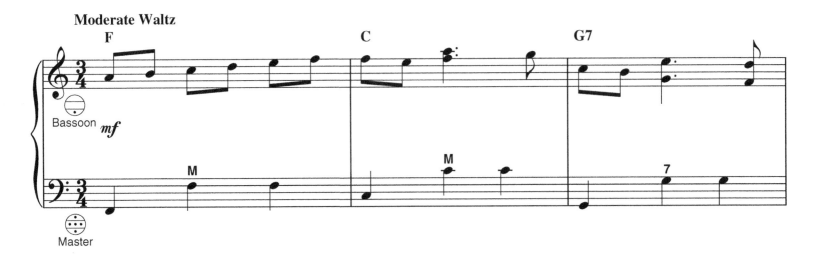

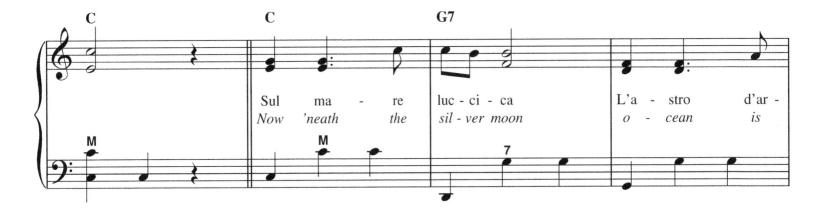

Sul ma - re luc - ci - ca L'a - stro d'ar -
Now 'neath the sil - ver moon o - cean is

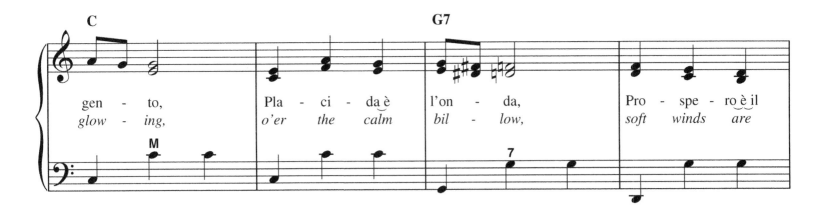

gen - to, Pla - ci - da è l'on - da, Pro - spe - ro è il
glow - ing, o'er the calm bil - low, soft winds are

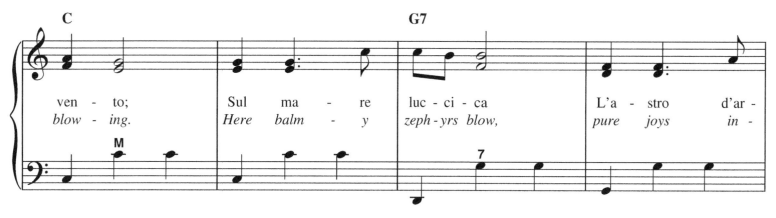

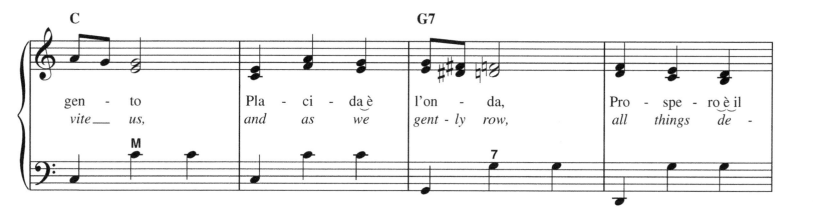

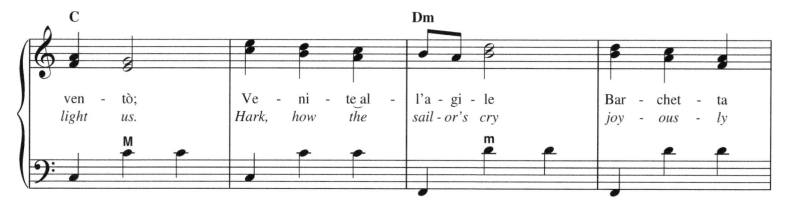

Santa Lu - ci - a!   Ve - ni - te al - l'a - gi - le
San - ta Lu - ci - a!   *Home of fair po - e - sy,*

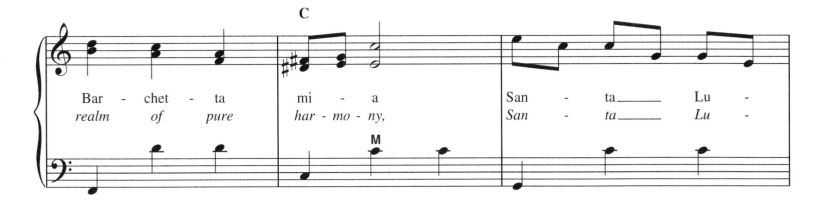

Bar - chet - ta   mi - a   San - ta Lu -
realm of pure   har - mo - ny,   San - ta Lu -

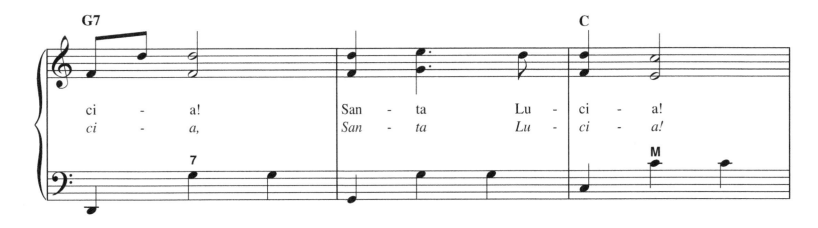

ci - a!   San - ta Lu - ci - a!
ci - a,   San - ta Lu - ci - a!

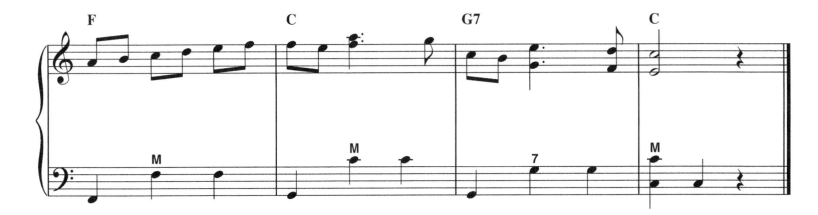

SHE'LL BE COMIN' 'ROUND THE MOUNTAIN

Traditional

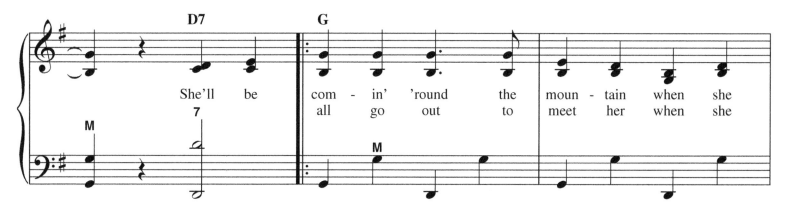

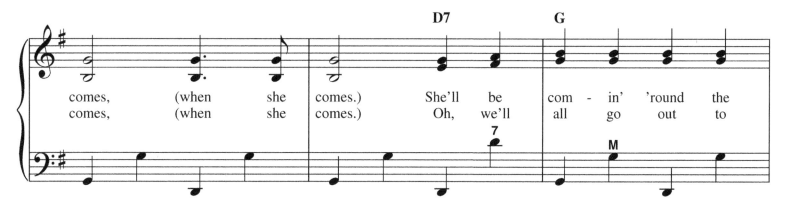

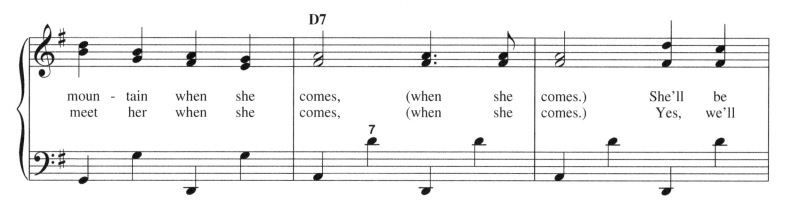

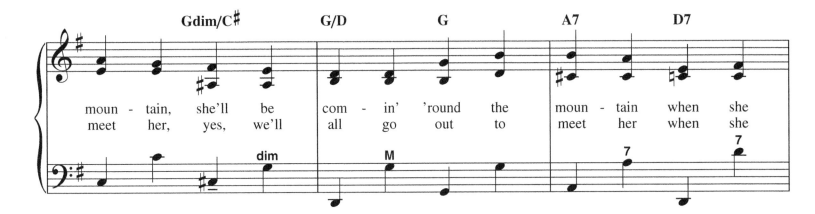

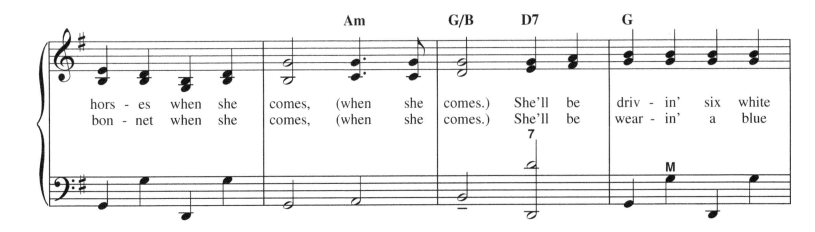

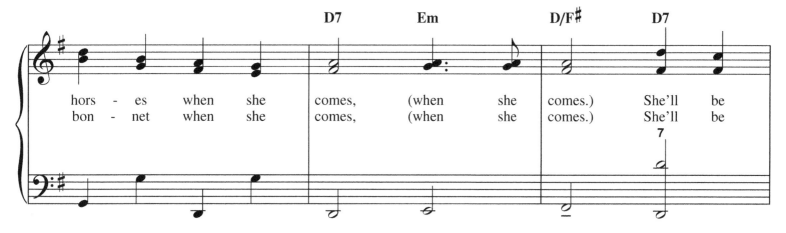

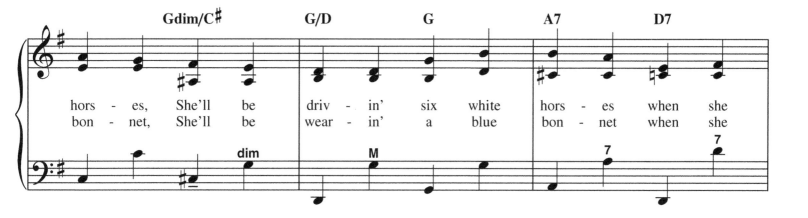

SWEET BETSY FROM PIKE

American Folksong

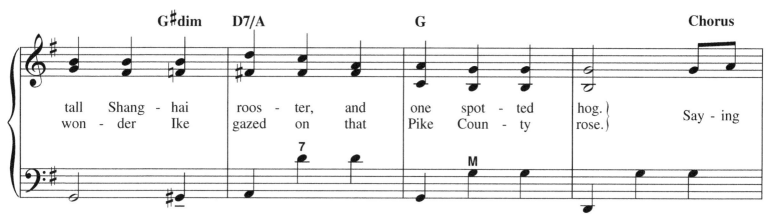

tall Shang - hai roos - ter, and one spot - ted hog. }
won - der Ike gazed on that Pike Coun - ty rose. }
Say - ing

good - bye, Pike Coun - ty, fare - well for a - while. We'll _

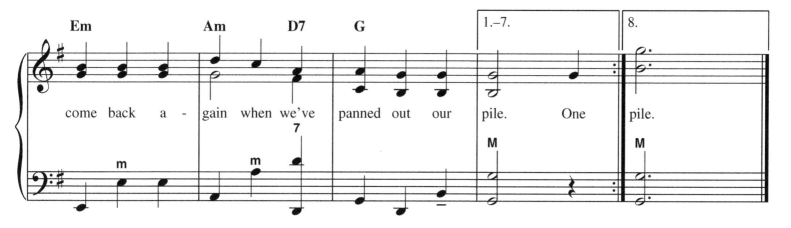

come back a - gain when we've panned out our pile. One pile.

Additional Lyrics

3. Their wagon broke down with a terrible crash,
   And out on the prairie rolled all kinds of trash,
   A few little baby clothes done up with care,
   'Twas rather suspicious, but all on the square.
   Chorus

4. The Shanghai ran off, and their cattle all died,
   That morning the last piece of bacon was fried,
   Poor Ike was discouraged and Betsy got mad,
   The dog dropped his tail and looked wondrously sad.
   Chorus

5. They soon reached the desert where Betsy gave out,
   And down in the sand she lay rolling about,
   While Ike, half distracted, looked on with surprise,
   Saying "Betsy, get up, you'll get sand in your eyes."
   Chorus

6. Sweet Betsy got up in a great deal of pain,
   Declared she'd go back to Pike County again,
   But Ike gave a sigh, and they fondly embraced
   And they traveled along with his arm 'round her waist.
   Chorus

7. They suddenly stopped on a very high hill,
   With wonder looked down upon old Placerville;
   Ike sighed when he said, and he cast his eyes down,
   "Sweet Betsy, my darling, we've got to Hangtown."
   Chorus

8. Long Ike and sweet Betsy attended a dance;
   Ike wore a pair of his Pike County pants;
   Sweet Betsy was dressed up in ribbons and rings;
   Says Ike, "You're an angel, but where are your wings?"
   Chorus

TARANTELLA

Traditional

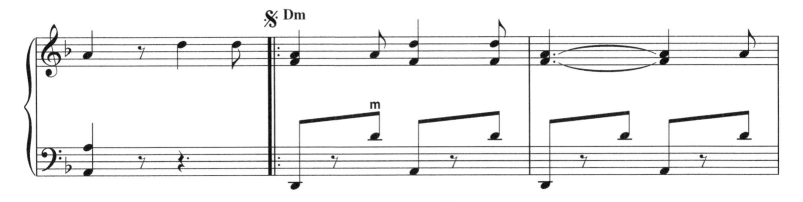

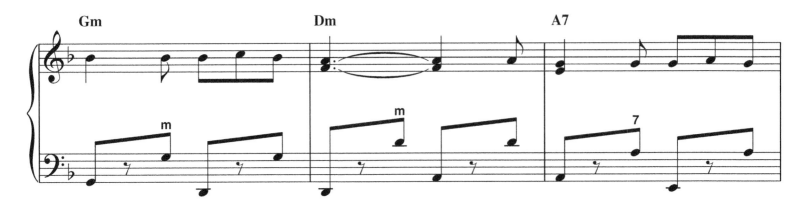

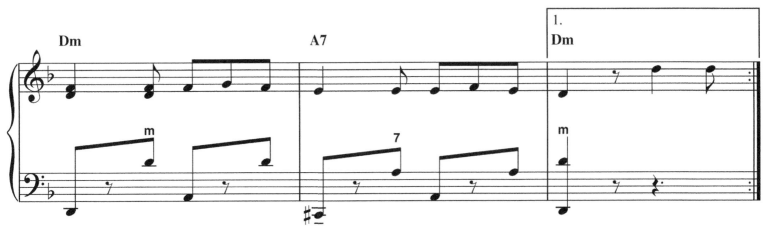

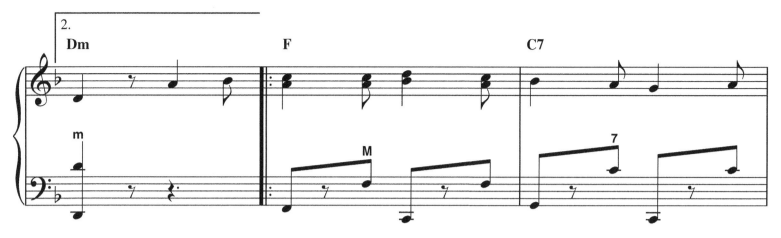

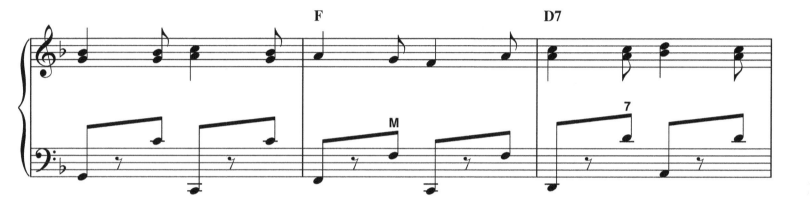

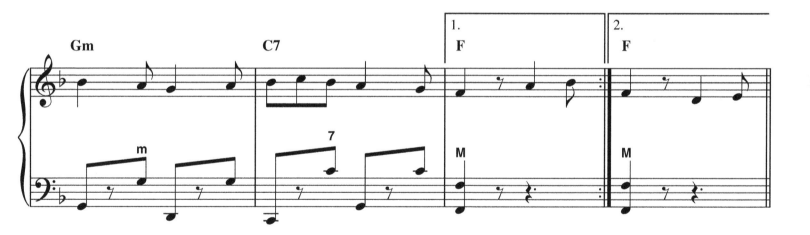

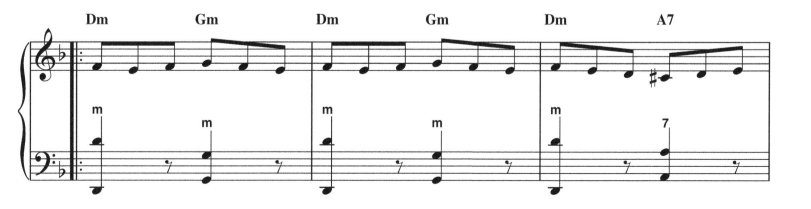

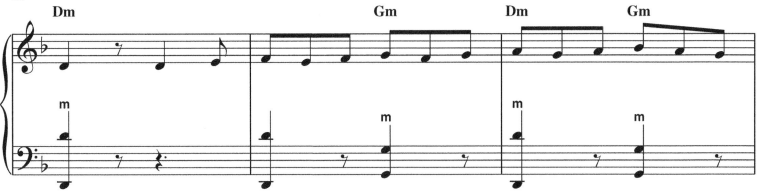

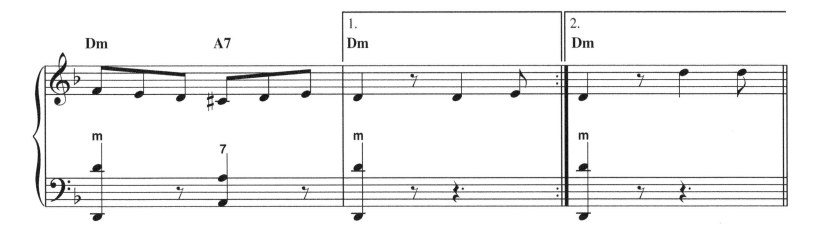

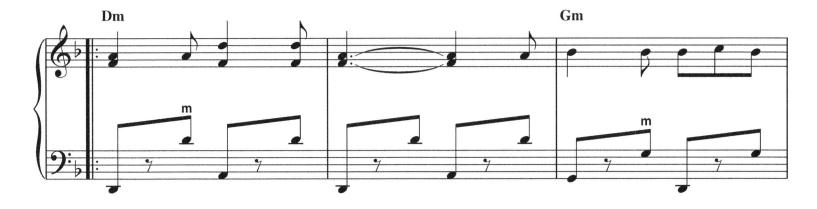

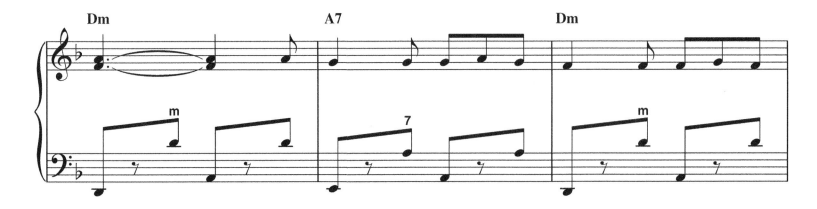

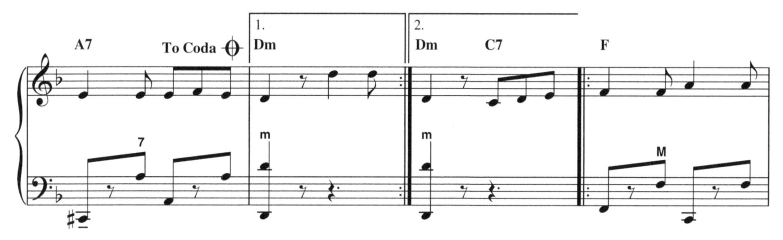

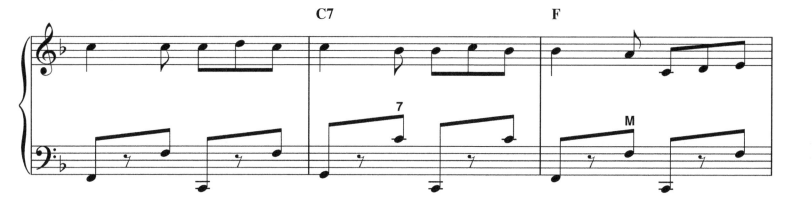

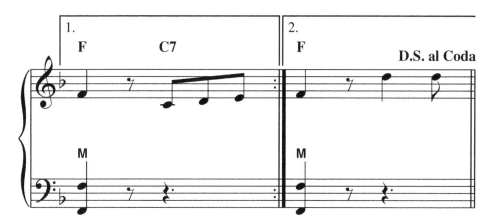

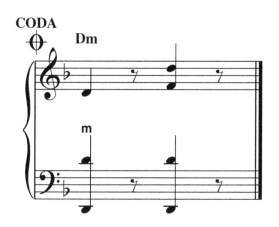

THERE IS A TAVERN IN THE TOWN

Traditional Drinking Song

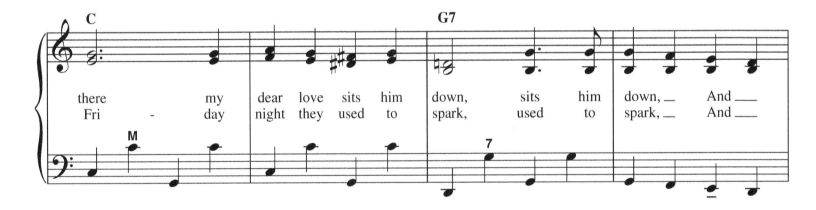

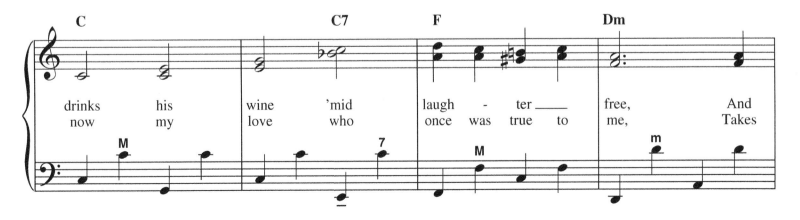

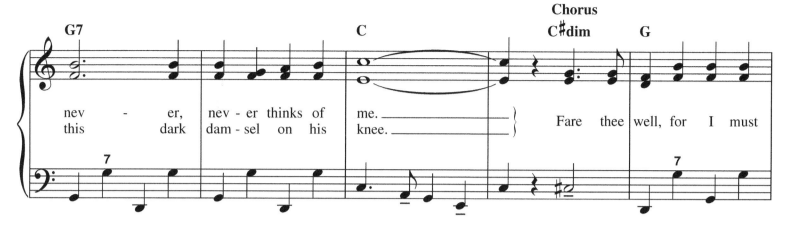

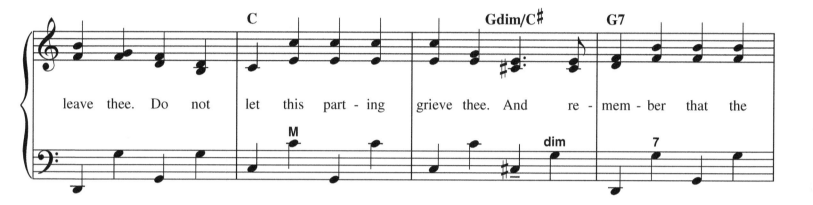

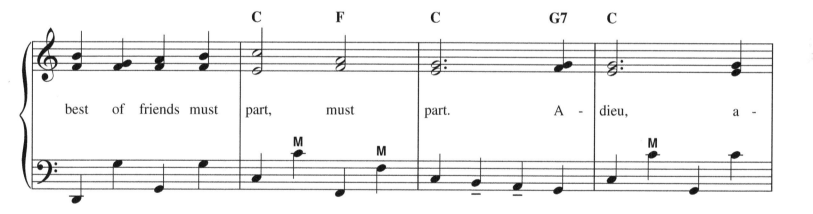

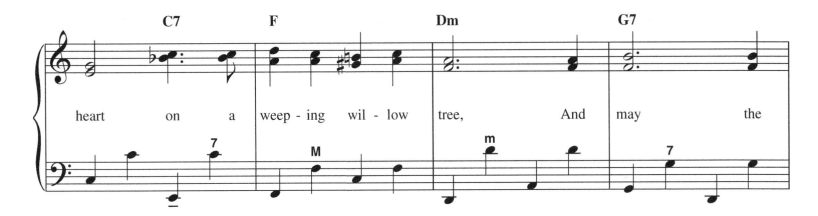

Additional Lyrics

3. And now I see him never more, never more.
   He never knocks upon my door, on my door.
   Oh, woe is me, he pinned a little note,
   And these were all the words he wrote:
   Chorus

4. Oh, dig my grave both wide and deep, wide and deep
   Put tombstones at my head and feet, head and feet.
   And on my breast you may carve a turtle dove,
   To signify I died for love.
   Chorus

TOM DOOLEY

Traditional Folksong

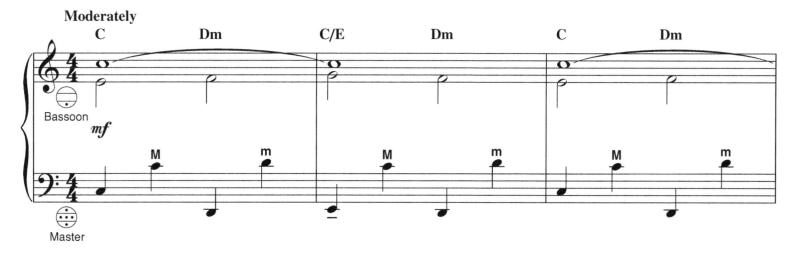

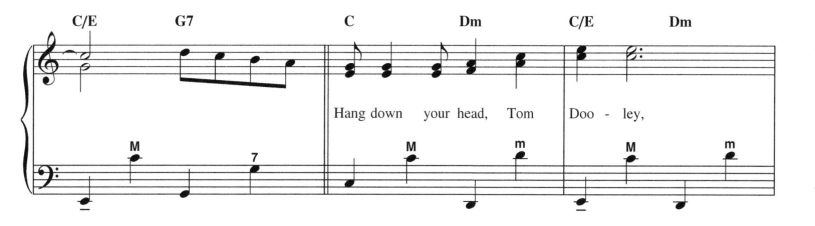

Hang down your head, Tom Doo - ley,

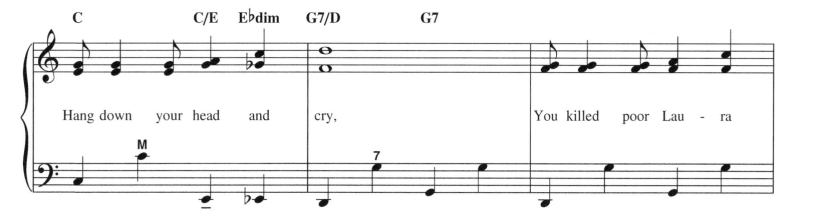

Hang down your head and cry, You killed poor Lau - ra

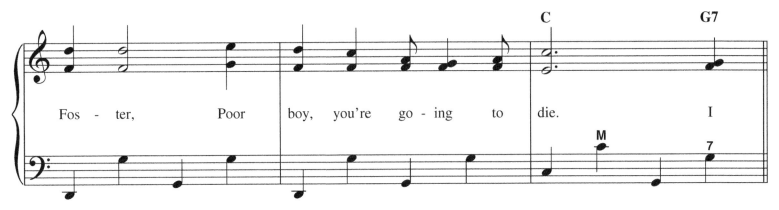

Fos - ter, Poor boy, you're go - ing to die. I

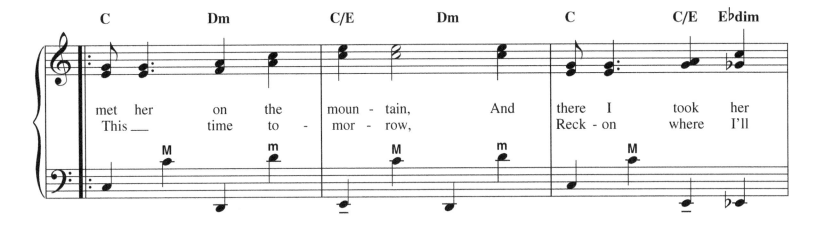

met her on the moun - tain, And there I took her
This ___ time to - mor - row, Reck - on where I'll

life. I met her on the moun - tain And I
be? In some lone - some val - ley A -

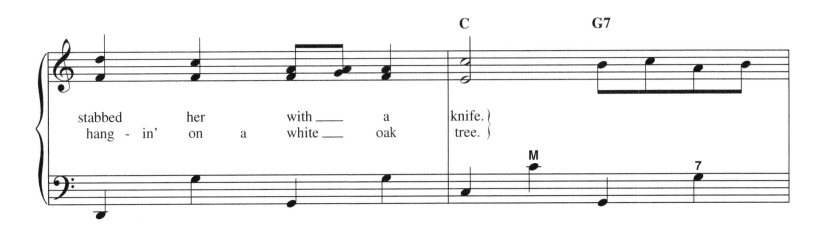

stabbed her with ___ a knife.
hang - in' on a white ___ oak tree.

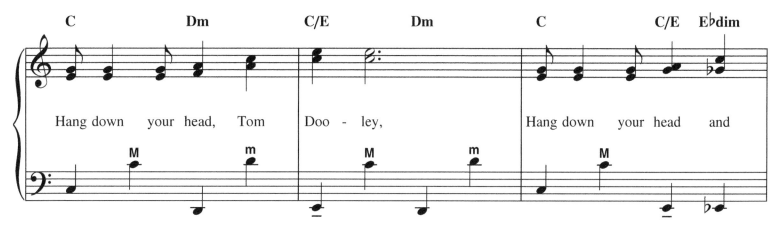

Hang down your head, Tom Doo - ley, Hang down your head and

cry, You killed poor Lau - ra Fos - ter, Poor

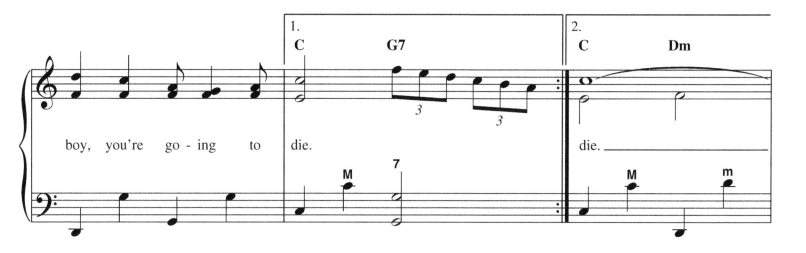

boy, you're go - ing to die. die.

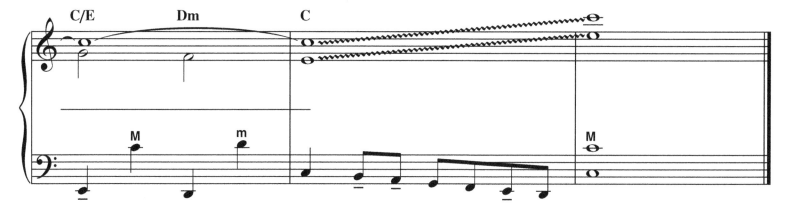

THE WABASH CANNON BALL

Hobo Song

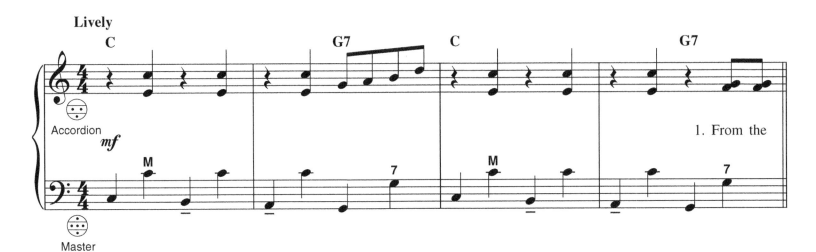

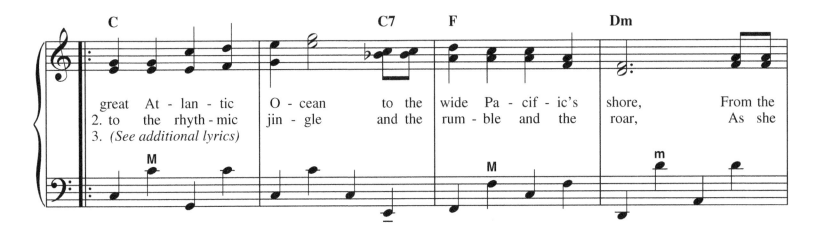

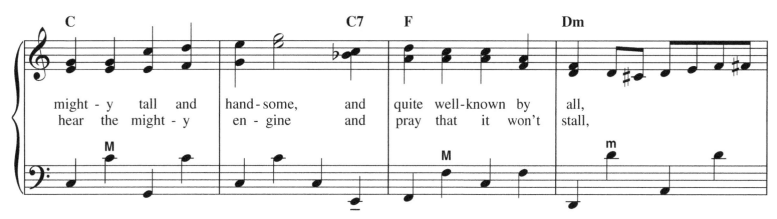

might - y tall and hand - some, and quite well-known by all,
hear the might - y en - gine and pray that it won't stall,

How we love the choo choo of the Wa - bash Can - non - ball.)
While we safe - ly trav - el on the Wa - bash Can - non - ball.) Hear the

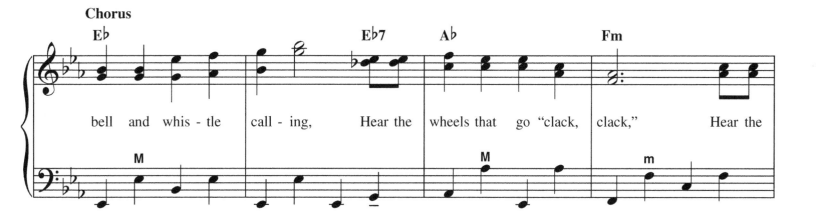

Chorus

bell and whis - tle call - ing, Hear the wheels that go "clack, clack," Hear the

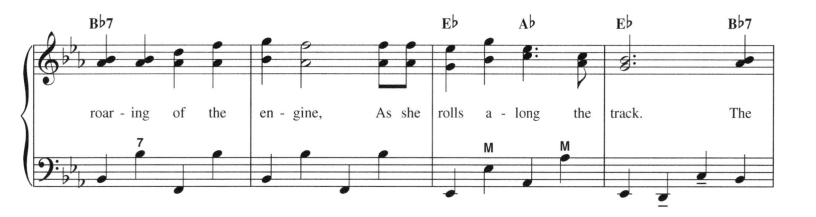

roar - ing of the en - gine, As she rolls a - long the track. The

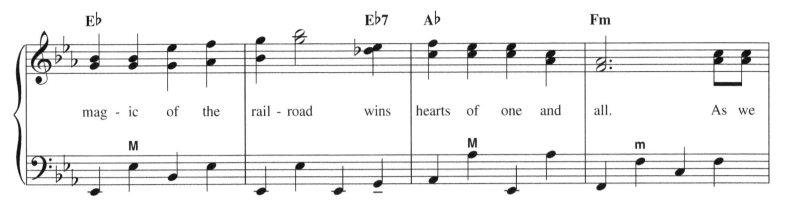

magic of the rail-road wins hearts of one and all. As we

reach our des-tin - a-tion on the Wa-bash Can-non - ball. { Lis-ten
{ She was

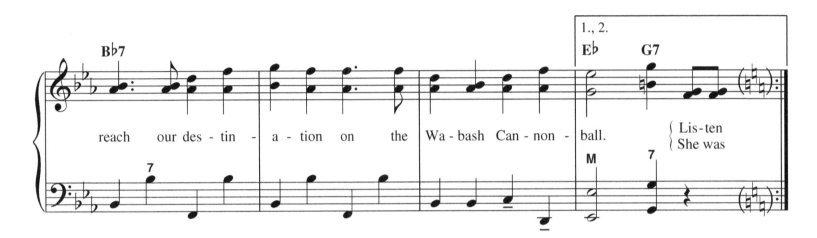

ball.

Additional Lyrics

3. She was coming from Atlanta on a cold December day.
As she rolled into the station, I could hear a woman say:
"He's mighty big and handsome, and sure did make me fall,
He's a coming tow'rd me on the Wabash Cannonball."
Chorus

YANKEE DOODLE

Traditional

1. Fa - ther and I went down to camp, A - long with Cap - tain
3. There _ was Cap - tain Wash - ing - ton up - on a slap - ping
5. *(See additional lyrics)*

Good - ing, and there we saw the men and boys as
stal - lion, a - giv - ing or - ders to his men, I

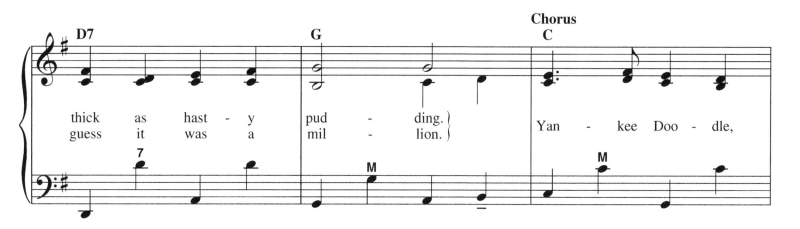

thick as hast - y pud - ding. }
guess it was a mil - lion. }

Chorus

Yan - kee Doo - dle,

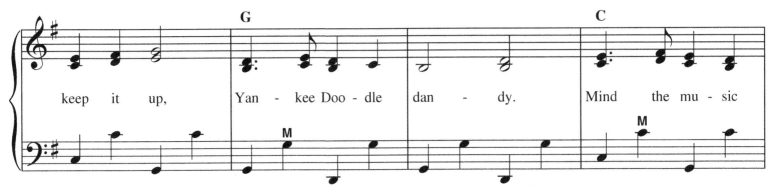

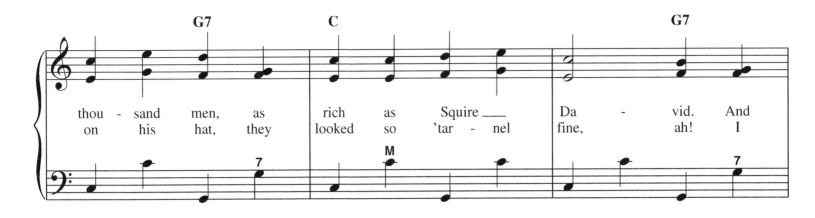

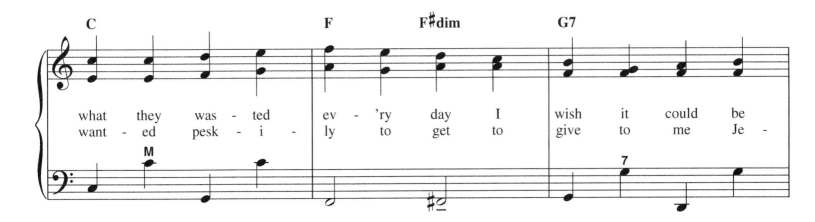

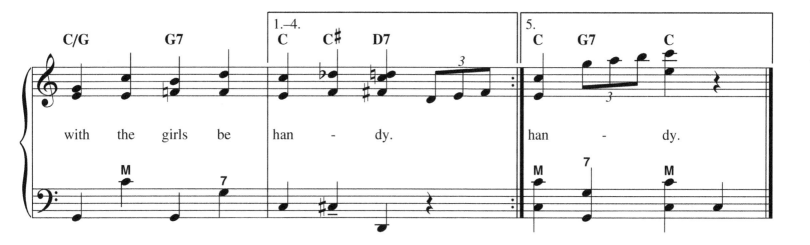

Additional Lyrics

5. We saw a little barrel too, the heads were made of leather.
They knocked on it with little clubs and called the folks together
Chorus

6. And there they'd fife away like fun, and play on cornstalk fiddles.
And some had ribbons red as blood all bound around their middles.
Chorus

WHEN JOHNNY COMES MARCHING HOME

Words and Music by
PATRICK SARSFIELD GILMORE

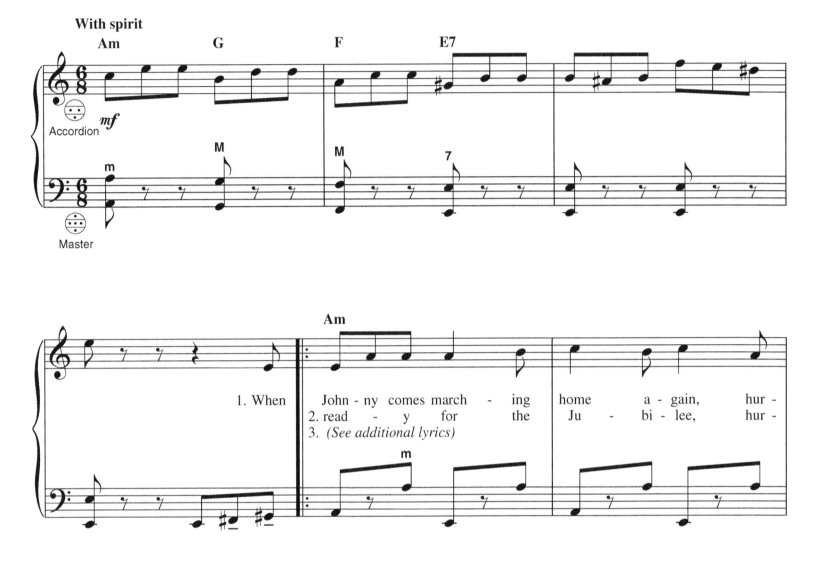

wel - come then, hur - rah! _____ Hur - rah! _____ Oh, the
three times three, hur - rah! _____ Hur - rah! _____ The __

men will cheer and the boys will shout. The la - dies they __ will
lau - rel wreath _ is read - y now to place up - on __ his

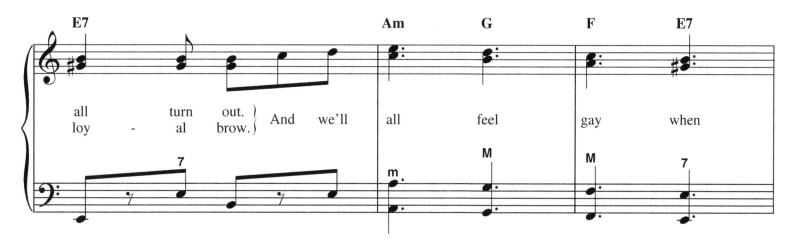

all turn out.
loy - al brow. } And we'll all feel gay when

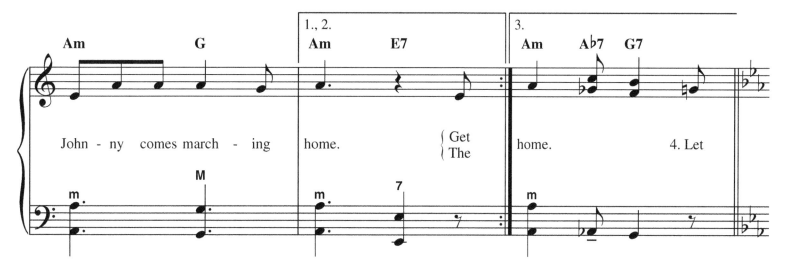

Johnny comes march - ing home. { Get home. 4. Let
{ The

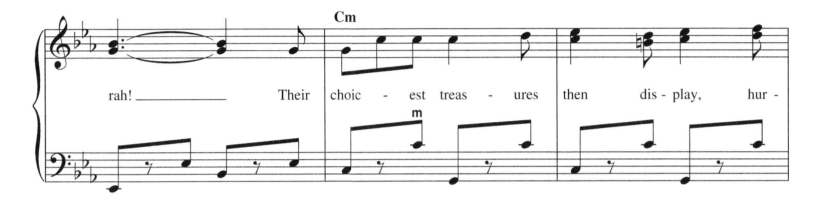

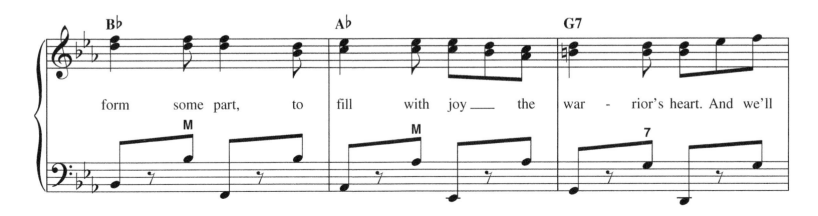

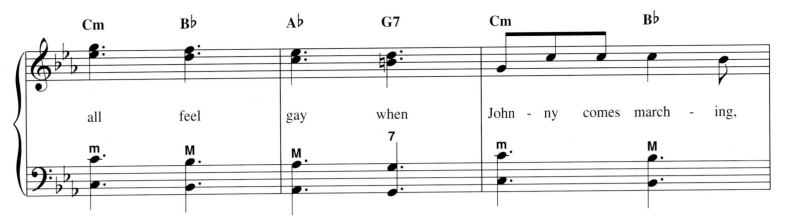

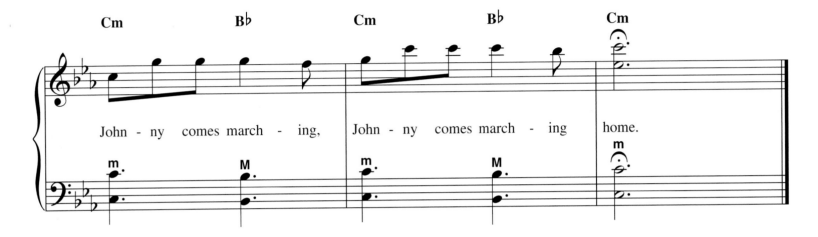

Additional Lyrics

3. The old church bell will peal with joy, hurrah, hurrah.
   To welcome home our darling boy, hurrah, hurrah.
   The village lads and lassies say with roses they will stew the way.
   And we'll all feel gay when Johnny comes marching home.

A COLLECTION OF ALL-TIME FAVORITES
FOR ACCORDION

ACCORDION FAVORITES
arr. Gary Meisner

16 all-time favorites, arranged for accordion, including: Can't Smile Without You • Could I Have This Dance • Endless Love • Memory • Sunrise, Sunset • I.O.U. • and more.
00359012...$12.99

ALL-TIME FAVORITES FOR ACCORDION
arr. Gary Meisner

20 must-know standards arranged for accordions. Includes: Ain't Misbehavin' • Autumn Leaves • Crazy • Hello, Dolly! • Hey, Good Lookin' • Moon River • Speak Softly, Love • Unchained Melody • The Way We Were • Zip-A-Dee-Doo-Dah • and more.
00311088...$12.99

THE BEATLES FOR ACCORDION

17 hits from the Lads from Liverpool have been arranged for accordion. Includes: All You Need Is Love • Eleanor Rigby • The Fool on the Hill • Here Comes the Sun • Hey Jude • In My Life • Let It Be • Ob-La-Di, Ob-La-Da • Penny Lane • When I'm Sixty-Four • Yesterday • and more.
00268724 ....$14.99

BROADWAY FAVORITES
arr. Ken Kotwitz

A collection of 17 wonderful show songs, including: Don't Cry for Me Argentina • Getting to Know You • If I Were a Rich Man • Oklahoma • People Will Say We're in Love • We Kiss in a Shadow.
00490157...$10.99

DISNEY SONGS FOR ACCORDION – 3RD EDITION

13 Disney favorites especially arranged for accordion, including: Be Our Guest • Beauty and the Beast • Can You Feel the Love Tonight • Chim Chim Cher-ee • It's a Small World • Let It Go • Under the Sea • A Whole New World • You'll Be in My Heart • Zip-A-Dee-Doo-Dah • and more!
00152508 ....$12.99

FIRST 50 SONGS YOU SHOULD PLAY ON THE ACCORDION
arr. Gary Meisner

If you're new to the accordion, you are probably eager to learn some songs. This book provides 50 simplified arrangements of must-know popular standards, folk songs and show tunes, including: All of Me • Beer Barrel Polka • Carnival of Venice • Edelweiss • Hava Nagila (Let's Be Happy) • Hernando's Hideaway • Jambalaya (On the Bayou) • Lady of Spain • Moon River • 'O Sole Mio • Sentimental Journey • Somewhere, My Love • That's Amore (That's Love) • Under Paris Skies • and more. Includes lyrics when applicable.
00250269 ....$16.99

FRENCH SONGS FOR ACCORDION
arr. Gary Meisner

A très magnifique collection of 17 French standards arranged for the accordion. Includes: Autumn Leaves • Beyond the Sea • C'est Magnifique • I Love Paris • La Marseillaise • Let It Be Me (Je T'appartiens) • Under Paris Skies • Watch What Happens • and more.
00311498...$10.99

HYMNS FOR ACCORDION
arr. Gary Meisner

24 treasured sacred favorites arranged for accordion, including: Amazing Grace • Beautiful Savior • Come, Thou Fount of Every Blessing • Crown Him with Many Crowns • Holy, Holy, Holy • It Is Well with My Soul • Just a Closer Walk with Thee • A Mighty Fortress Is Our God • Nearer, My God, to Thee • The Old Rugged Cross • Rock of Ages • What a Friend We Have in Jesus • and more.
00277160 ....$9.99

ITALIAN SONGS FOR ACCORDION
arr. Gary Meisner

17 favorite Italian standards arranged for accordion, including: Carnival of Venice • Ciribiribin • Come Back to Sorrento • Funiculi, Funicula • La donna è mobile • La Spagnola • 'O Sole Mio • Santa Lucia • Tarantella • and more.
00311089...$9.95

LATIN FAVORITES FOR ACCORDION
arr. Gary Meisner

20 Latin favorites, including: Bésame Mucho (Kiss Me Much) • The Girl from Ipanema • How Insensitive (Insensatez) • Perfidia • Spanish Eyes • So Nice (Summer Samba) • and more.
00310932...$14.99

THE FRANK MAROCCO ACCORDION SONGBOOK

This songbook includes arrangements and recordings of 15 standards and original songs from legendary jazz accordionist Frank Marocco, including: All the Things You Are • Autumn Leaves • Beyond the Sea • Moon River • Moonlight in Vermont • Stormy Weather (Keeps Rainin' All the Time) • and more!
00233441 Book/Online Audio...............$19.99

POP STANDARDS FOR ACCORDION
Arrangements of 20 Classic Songs

20 classic pop standards arranged for accordion are included in this collection: Annie's Song • Chances Are • For Once in My Life • Help Me Make It Through the Night • My Cherie Amour • Ramblin' Rose • (Sittin' On) The Dock of the Bay • That's Amore (That's Love) • Unchained Melody • and more.
00254822 ....$14.99

POLKA FAVORITES
arr. Kenny Kotwitz

An exciting new collection of 16 songs, including: Beer Barrel Polka • Liechtensteiner Polka • My Melody of Love • Paloma Blanca • Pennsylvania Polka • Too Fat Polka • and more.
00311573...$12.99

STAR WARS FOR ACCORDION

A dozen songs from the Star Wars franchise: The Imperial March (Darth Vader's Theme) • Luke and Leia • March of the Resistance • Princess Leia's Theme • Rey's Theme • Star Wars (Main Theme) • and more.
00157380 ....$14.99

TANGOS FOR ACCORDION
arr. Gary Meisner

Every accordionist needs to know some tangos! Here are 15 favorites: Amapola (Pretty Little Poppy) • Aquellos Ojos Verdes (Green Eyes) • Hernando's Hideaway • Jalousie (Jealousy) • Kiss of Fire • La Cumparsita (The Masked One) • Quizás, Quizás, Quizás (Perhaps, Perhaps, Perhaps) • The Rain in Spain • Tango of Roses • Whatever Lola Wants (Lola Gets) • and more!
00122252 ....$9.99

3-CHORD SONGS FOR ACCORDION
arr. Gary Meisner

Here are nearly 30 songs that are easy to play but still sound great! Includes: Amazing Grace • Can Can • Danny Boy • For He's a Jolly Good Fellow • He's Got the Whole World in His Hands • Just a Closer Walk with Thee • La Paloma Blanca (The White Dove) • My Country, 'Tis of Thee • Ode to Joy • Oh! Susanna • Yankee Doodle • The Yellow Rose of Texas • and more.
00312104 ....$12.99

LAWRENCE WELK'S POLKA FOLIO

More than 50 famous polkas, schottisches and waltzes arranged for piano and accordion, including: Blue Eyes • Budweiser Polka • Clarinet Polka • Cuckoo Polka • The Dove Polka • Draw One Polka • Gypsy Polka • Helena Polka • International Waltzes • Let's Have Another One • Schnitzelbank • Shuffle Schottische • Squeeze Box Polka • Waldteuful Waltzes • and more.
00123218...$12.99

HAL•LEONARD®
Visit Hal Leonard Online at
www.halleonard.com

HAL•LEONARD ACCORDION PLAY•ALONG

The Accordion Play-Along series features custom accordion arrangements with CD tracks recorded by a live band (accordion, bass and drums). There are two audio tracks for each song – a full performance for listening, plus a separate backing track which lets you be the soloist! The CD is playable on any CD player, and is also enhanced so Mac and PC users can adjust the recording to any tempo without changing the pitch!

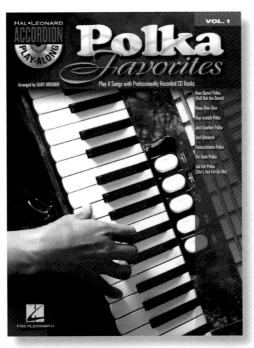

1. POLKA FAVORITES
arr. Gary Meisner
Beer Barrel Polka (Roll Out the Barrel) • Hoop-Dee-Doo • Hop-scotch Polka • Just Another Polka • Just Because • Pennsylvania Polka • Tic-Tock Polka • Too Fat Polka (She's Too Fat for Me).
00701705 Book/CD Pack.. $14.99

2. ALL-TIME HITS
arr. Gary Meisner
Edelweiss • Fly Me to the Moon (In Other Words) • I Left My Heart in San Francisco • It's a Small World • Moon River • More (Ti Guarderò Nel Cuore) • Poinciana (Song of the Tree) • When I'm Sixty-Four.
00701706 Book/CD Pack.. $14.99

3. CLASSIC SONGS
arr. Gary Meisner
Carnival of Venice • Ciribiribin • Come Back to Sorrento • Fascination (Valse Tzigane) • Funiculi, Funicula • I Love You Truly • In the Good Old Summertime • Melody of Love • Peg O' My Heart • When Irish Eyes Are Smiling.
00701707 Book/CD Pack.. $14.99

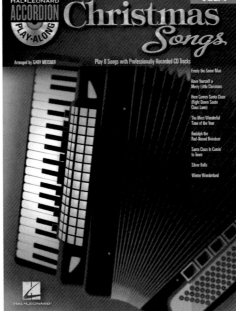

4. CHRISTMAS SONGS
arr. Gary Meisner
Frosty the Snow Man • Have Yourself a Merry Little Christmas • Here Comes Santa Claus (Right down Santa Claus Lane) • The Most Wonderful Time of the Year • Rudolph the Red-Nosed Reindeer • Santa Claus Is Comin' to Town • Silver Bells • Winter Wonderland.
00101770 Book/CD Pack.. $14.99

5. ITALIAN SONGS
arr. Gary Meisner
La Sorella • La Spagnola • Mattinata • 'O Sole Mio • Oh Marie • Santa Lucia • Tarantella • Vieni Sul Mar.
00101771 Book/CD Pack.. $14.99

HAL•LEONARD®

Visit Hal Leonard online at **www.halleonard.com**

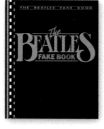

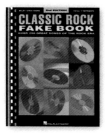

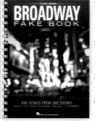

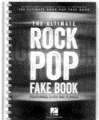